COLLECTOR'S VALUE GUIDE™

Department 56®

Snowbabies™

Snowbunnies® *Easter Collectibles*

Collector Handbook and Secondary Market Price Guide

FOURTH EDITION

Snowbabies™

Managing Editor:	Jeff Mahony	Creative Director:	Joe T. Nguyen
Associate Editors:	Melissa A. Bennett	Production Supervisor:	Scott Sierakowski
	Jan Cronan	Senior Graphic Designers:	Lance Doyle
	Gia C. Manalio		Susannah C. Judd
	Paula Stuckart		David S. Maloney
Contributing Editor:	Mike Micciulla		Carole Mattia-Slater
Editorial Assistants:	Timothy R. Affleck	Graphic Designers:	Jennifer J. Bennett
	Heather N. Carreiro		Sean-Ryan Dudley
	Jennifer Filipek		Kimberly Eastman
	Beth Hackett		Jason C. Jasch
	Nicole LeGard Lenderking		Angi Shearstone
	Steven Shinkaruk		David Ten Eyck
	Joan C. Wheal	Art Interns:	Huy Hoang
Web Reporters:	Samantha Bouffard		Anna Zagajewska
	Ren Messina	Web Graphic Designer:	Ryan Falis
		Product Development Manager:	Paul Rasid
		R&D Specialist:	Priscilla Berthiaume

ISBN 1-888-914-85-8

CheckerBee
PUBLISHING

306 Industrial Park Road • Middletown, CT 06457
www.collectorbee.com

Table Of Contents

Introducing The Collector's Value Guide™

W elcome to the fourth edition of the Collector's Value Guide™ to Snowbabies™, Snowbunnies® and Easter Collectible figurines from Department 56®, Inc.!

This edition of the Collector's Value Guide™ is an invaluable source for the most up-to-date secondary market information for your entire collection. The full-color value guide section will help you keep track of the current value and size of your collection, as well as provide issue and retirement dates, and original prices.

Whether you are a long-time Snowbabies collector or have just purchased your first piece, the Collector's Value Guide™ will become your constant companion as you make the enjoyable journey through Frosty Frolic Land™.

Look Inside To Find:

✳ The history of the Snowbabies designs, from European customs to today's collection from Department 56

✳ A biography of Snowbabies designer Kristi Jensen Pierro

✳ Collector stories from Snowbabies fans across the country

✳ A close-up look at the new Snowbabies pieces for 2000

✳ Display ideas for showcasing your Snowbabies collection

✳ A gift category checklist to help you select appropriate Snowbabies pieces for your friends and loved ones

The Snowbabies™ Story

Department 56 has enchanted collectors for more than a decade with delightful designs of Snowbabies. Styled to resemble angelic babies dressed in white, frosted snowsuits, these figurines are actually based on 19th-century Christmas treats and a baby born in Greenland – a child so fair that the Eskimos believed she was made of snow! Knowing the background and history of these charming babies make them even more endearing.

Sugar Dolls & Tree Sweets

Historians believe that the original "snow baby" design dates back to the early 1800s and a German holiday tradition. In celebration of Twelfth Night – the night that the the three wise men brought gifts to baby Jesus – small sweet cakes were served after decorating them as "Zuckerpuppen" (sugar dolls), which were miniature images of the Christ child made of flour and sugar or marzipan, an almond-flavored paste. Other ornamental sugar babies known as "Tannenbaumkonfekt" (fir tree confection) were made and hung on Christmas trees. By the mid 1800s, the popularity of these holiday decorations led to the production of reusable and durable porcelain figures.

The Peary Connection

Other experts offer an American contribution to the snow babies' beginnings with the tale of an infant born in 1893 to an American couple living in Greenland. Until that time, this desolate and forbidding polar region was only inhabited by dark-skinned native Eskimos, but explorer Robert Peary, his wife and others were there on an expedition in search of the North Pole. Josephine Peary had already made history in 1891 by being the first white woman to spend a winter season in

this hostile environment, but when she gave birth to her daughter, news of a "snowbaby" spread throughout the settlements and Eskimos traveled to see this white-skinned child. Marie Ahnighito Peary was called "Ah-poo-mick-ananny" by the natives, which means "snowbaby."

The Porcelain Babies

Whatever truly inspired the first snowbaby design, these porcelain figures of babies dressed in white parkas covered with "snow" were made in Germany at the turn of the 20th century, and exported to America. Made of a hand-whipped bisque that was poured into molds, these babies were originally dressed in all-white outfits, but eventually wore colored shoes and were seated on sleds, standing on skis and engaged in a variety of fun-filled outdoor activities. After the birth of the Peary's second child, figures of two snowbabies began appearing together on sleds or hugging each other. By the 1930s, Japanese-produced snowbabies joined the German designs, which are all sought by antique collectors today.

What A Great Idea!

circa 1910

1987

These collectible snowbabies caught the eye of Bill Kirchner, an avid antique hunter and, at the time, vice president of product development and advertising at Department 56, Inc. Charmed by the rough bisque finish of these playful figures, Kirchner brought samples to work and, with the assistance of artist Kristi Jensen Pierro, developed the original designs for the Department 56 Snowbabies collection. Introduced in 1986, the line was distributed to stores in 1987. Pierro reproduced many of the original designs, to the delight of Snowbabies collectors. The babies' innocent expressions charm those who appreciate both the old and the new.

Collectors Fall In Love

After the first 16 Snowbabies were issued – which included light-up, clip-on ornaments; waterglobes; music box designs; and accessory trees – the introduction of limited edition pieces, polar bears, penguins and puffins added to the line's popularity and desirability. Larger figurines, such as grandfatherly "Jack Frost," were introduced in 1994, in addition to the pastel-colored Snowbunnies. Also that year, the first human figure in Frosty Frolic Land, Crystal, made her debut in Department 56's children's book "Winter Tales of Snowbabies™." This charming story explains how the world in which the Snowbabies live can be found in every tiny snowflake that drifts down from the sky. Crystal, the young girl who discovered these miniature Snowbabies, has since

appeared in each club member exclusive figurine since the debut of the Snowbabies Friendship Club™ in 1997.

In the past decade, Department 56 has released and retired Snowbabies pieces annually; the collection now includes more than 300 pieces, including figurines, ornaments, waterglobes, music boxes and other accessory pieces. The Snowbunnies collection has multiplied to more than 80 versions of bisque bunnies, and a pair of Easter Collectible animal figurines has been released each year since 1990 to celebrate the Easter season.

Guests In Frosty Frolic Land

Department 56 recently introduced two special Snowbabies series that set them apart in design and theme. L. Frank Baum's timeless tale of courage, ruby slippers, and little people, "The Wonderful Wizard Of Oz" was first published in 1900. The memorable characters from the story have been honored as featured visitors to Frosty Frolic Land in the first piece in The Guest Collection™, released in 1998: "I Have A Feeling We're Not In Kansas Anymore." A second Oz figurine, issued in 1999, features Dorothy with her friends the Cowardly Lion, the Scarecrow and the Tin Man: "They're Coming From Oz, Oh My!"

Another character from a familiar literary classic is featured in the 1999 Snowbabies figurine "A Gift So Fine From Madeline." Author Ludwig Bemelmans introduced the Parisian girl in 1939 with a series of Madeline books. Since then, her adventures have taken her to London and, eventually, to America.

Tweety Bird, the animated yellow canary, made his debut in a 1942 cartoon and uttered the now familiar line, "I tawt I taw a puddy-tat." The Snowbabies figurine "A Kiss For You And 2000 Too" features the familiar Looney Tunes character as he welcomes the millennium with Snowbabies friends from Frosty Frolic Land.

Snowbabies Take Up Sports

New for 2000 is a quartet of athletically-fit participants of the *Snowbabies Starlight Games*™ who personify the spirit of athletic competition, camaraderie and teamwork. These Snowbabies are involved in the sports of vault jumping, diving, soccer and baseball, and are depicted in the pieces "Over The Top," "Hit The Mark," "Score" and "Batter Up."

Now, it's time to introduce you to the artist who brings all the Snowbabies pieces to life with four simple guidelines: the Snowbabies are neither boys or girls – just babies; their titles are self explanatory; each character is pictured in realistic situations (the babies do "baby things" and the animals do "animal things"); and every piece reflects the innocence of childhood. The artist is Kristi Jensen Pierro, and here is her story . . .

Meet Kristi Jensen Pierro

K risti Jensen Pierro is the creator behind the delightful faces of the Department 56 Snowbabies and Snowbunnies lines. Although she never lived in the frozen North Pole, Pierro did grow up in cold Minnesota. An avid illustrator, Pierro graduated in 1979 from St. Cloud (Minn.) State University with a degree in fine arts. Her association with Department 56 began shortly after graduation when she accepted a position as a free-lance artist.

Bill Kirchner, who was then the vice president of product development and advertising at Department 56, brought the idea of a snow baby line to the company in the early 1980s. Pierro joined him in designing and developing the original concept, her first assignment as a full-time designer and illustrator for the company. Much of the line's success has been due to Pierro's ability to inject life and whimsy into her snowsuited babies' designs.

Pierro has used her two young daughters as models. "In fact, these kids have posed so many times that I wonder if they actually think of themselves as Snowbabies," Pierro said recently in an interview. The piece "You Are My Lucky Star" was inspired by her children's love of music, while other pieces are based on Pierro's childhood memories. Her children aren't the only family members represented in bisque porcelain and crystal. The family dog has been transformed into the polar bear on many Snowbabies pieces, and Pierro's husband was the inspiration for the "grandfatherly figure" of Jack Frost.

No matter where she gets her inspiration, one thing is sure. As long as Kristi Jensen Pierro keeps creating Snowbabies designs, enthusiastic collectors will continue welcoming them into their hearts and homes.

Collector Stories

Snowbabies, Snowbunnies and Easter Collectible figurines are some of today's most popular collectibles. In this section, fans from around the country share their thoughts and special moments about their beloved pieces and what makes them so special.

Dyanna has always loved snow and children. "Combine the two and you have Snowbabies, the perfect collectible," she says. In addition to Snowbabies figurines and miniatures, she also collects postcards and dealer collectibles, and she has made a scrapbook so that her collection can be handed down to future generations, which includes her first granddaughter, Mollie.

The Snowbabies figurine that Genny and her husband, Ken, received from her mother as a wedding gift four years ago sat alone for a while before the "spirit" of the Snowbabies caught them. For their first anniversary, Ken bought two more pieces and the rest is history. "You never know where the road to 'nubbie land' will lead," Ken says, "and we have met some great people along the way."

There are two Snowbabies collectors in Dale and Mazelle's home. Dale says his favorite piece, "Jack Frost . . . A Touch Of Winter's Magic," represents what the Snowbabies are all about. "You can just see him looking out over the scene with all the babies as they are playing," says Dale. "He is the grandfather figure who has all these grandchildren and they know they can get away with almost anything!"

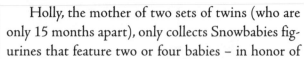

Holly, the mother of two sets of twins (who are only 15 months apart), only collects Snowbabies figurines that feature two or four babies – in honor of her twins. Her collection has grown to about 40 pieces, so Holly now displays her pieces year-round and not just during the winter season. The figurine that started it all was "Winter Surprise!" – a gift box with two Snowbabies peeking out from under the cover.

You never know who you might be competing against for that special Snowbabies figurine! Penny was bidding for "Mickey's New Friend" on an Internet auction site and was unknowingly bidding against a friend in New Jersey. Only through a phone call did they find out that they were in competition! It turns out that neither of them obtained that specific Snowbabies piece, but both of them eventually located other editions to call their own.

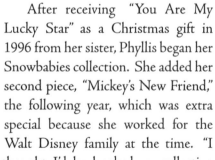

After receiving "You Are My Lucky Star" as a Christmas gift in 1996 from her sister, Phyllis began her Snowbabies collection. She added her second piece, "Mickey's New Friend," the following year, which was extra special because she worked for the Walt Disney family at the time. "I never thought I'd be hooked on collecting anything," Phyllis says. "It must be magic!"

Ellen's Snowbabies collection was growing with gifts from relatives until her husband discovered there were animals in some of the figurines. "That was the day it became *our* collection," she says. Now, when they get a new piece, they have a "discussion" about who gets to place it in one of their various displays, which are in every room of their house – except the children's bedrooms!

Katherine started her granddaughter's Snowbabies collection when Jenna was five and admired her grandmother's Snowbabies figurines. Katherine wanted to establish a collecting connection with

Jenna, and it has continued for five years. Jenna receives a figurine as a gift from her grandmother on special days throughout the year – and there always seems to be an appropriate piece for every occasion.

Sue inherited ten snowbabies and snow animals from her mother, who years ago had bought them for 10 to 25 cents each and displayed them at Christmas time. "My mother died when I was five, and these little babies are all that I have of her," Sue says. But one year, Sue couldn't find the treasures and was heartbroken. She found them years later in the attic, but in the meantime, her daughter had given her several Department 56 Snowbabies, including "Tumbling In The Snow." "When I came across the pewter Snowbabies, I was in seventh heaven," says Sue, "because they were almost the same size as my old ones!"

What's New For 2000

This section highlights the new Snowbabies releases for Spring 2000, including a new piece in The Guest Collection and the first four members of the *Snowbabies Starlight Games*, which makes its debut in 2000.

❄ Snowbabies Figurines ❄

BATTER UP (SNOWBABIES STARLIGHT GAMES). . . The *Snowbabies Starlight Games* is a special event held in Frosty Frolic Land that celebrates both teamwork and physical achievement. America's favorite pastime, the game of baseball, is honored in this series piece.

COME SAIL WITH ME . . . Three Snowbabies enjoy an afternoon sail on the lake with their penguin friend who is perched on the bow, keeping watch.

EVEN A SMALL LIGHT SHINES IN THE DARKNESS . . . With the lead Snowbaby holding a shining lantern, three more are doing their best to follow, with some comical consequences!

FALLING FOR YOU . . . Featuring a cubic base of clear acrylic, this cherubic Snowbaby is defying gravity to offer its heart and capture yours!

A GIFT FOR YOU (AVON EXCLUSIVES) . . .
These Snowbabies figurines each hold a gift box displaying a Swarovski crystal that represents a monthly birthstone. Choose from these 12: Garnet (January), Amethyst (February), Aquamarine (March), Diamond (April), Emerald (May), Pearl (June), Ruby (July), Peridot (August), Sapphire (September), Opal (October), Topaz (November) or Turquoise (December).

HIT THE MARK (SNOWBABIES STARLIGHT GAMES) . . .
Diving is instinctive to penguins so this perfect coach offers some advice to an aspiring Snowbaby competitor at the Starlight Games.

I'LL LOVE YOU ALWAYS (SPRING PROMOTION EVENT PIECE) . . . The Discover Department 56 Spring Promotion features this heartwarming piece that spotlights the unconditional love between parent and child.

JACK FROST . . . THROUGH THE FROST FOREST . . .
Two Snowbabies escort old Jack Frost into their homeland as a friendly moose provides the mode of transportation.

JOLLY FRIENDS FOREVERMORE (SET/11) . . . The bond of friendship is evident in this set, featuring two Snowbabies, a snowman and two smaller comrades. Also included are five sisal trees and a bag of snow to make your display complete.

JUMPING FOR JOY... Pure joy radiates on the face of this Snowbaby who is caught in mid-air during a leap of exhilaration!

THE LITTLEST ANGEL . . . The first angel in the Snowbabies family, this little charmer's halo hovers above it's hooded head.

MUSIC FROM THE HIGHEST (SET/3) . . . Three musically talented Snowbabies are all tuned up and ready to make any announcement a festive one!

OVER THE TOP (SNOWBABIES STARLIGHT GAMES) ... A polar bear patiently stands in for the vaulting horse during the Starlight Games as this champion athlete shows perfect form.

SCORE (SNOWBABIES STARLIGHT GAMES) ... In position to score the winning goal, this Snowbaby proudly represents the athletes in Frosty Frolic Land.

SHAKE IT UP, BABY ... Holding a miniature waterglobe – the first Snowbabies to do so – this baby watches as the snow swirls around the snowman inside.

STARLIGHT, STARBRIGHT ... Gazing upon the star dangling above its head, a Snowbaby contemplates the perfect wish.

THEY'RE COMING FROM OZ, OH MY! (THE GUEST COLLECTION) ... The fourth piece in The Guest Collection, this figurine features three curious Snowbabies peering into a crystal ball with visitors from Oz – Dorothy, Toto, the Scarecrow, the Cowardly Lion and the Tin Man.

❄ Ornaments ❄

BEST FRIENDS ... This miniature ornament illustrates the close relationship shared between these two best friends – the Snowbaby and the penguin.

MOONDREAMS & HANGIN' ON (SET/2) ... In this two-piece set, two Snowbabies are sitting on and slipping off glazed crescent moons.

THEY CALL ME JOYFUL ... Juggling the letters J–O–Y in its arms, this miniature Snowbaby brings a message of cheer.

❄ Musicals & Waterglobes ❄

MAKE A WISH . . . The secret wish that is furtively made before the candle flame is extinguished is immortalized in this musical waterglobe that plays "Happy Birthday To You."

SHIP O'DREAMS . . . This popular design of Snowbabies sailing their ship to dreamland is captured in a waterglobe that features a blowing snow switch.

THAT'S WHAT FRIENDS ARE FOR . . . An igloo is built as the husky snoozes in its doorway and the tune "That's What Friends Are For" accompanies the activity.

❄ Hinged Boxes ❄

REACH OUT . . . Look for the name of the box inside this piece, which is the first-ever hinged Snowbabies box to feature a waterglobe.

SENDING HUGS TO YOU (SPRING PROMOTION EVENT PIECE) . . . Making sure that their hugs and kisses are sent along posthaste, these two friends are keeping an eye on their special delivery!

SUPER STAR . . . Perched on one of the star's points, a Snowbaby waits for you to hide a wish or two inside this uniquely shaped hinged box.

TAKE THE FIRST STEP . . . This is not where you would expect a Snowbaby to be hiding, but this one has found the perfect fit in this hinged box design.

Pewter Miniatures

ALL ABOARD THE STAR EXPRESS (SET/4) . . . Remember when you were young and imagined that a couple of empty boxes were a train? These Snowbabies and their penguin friend in their imaginary choo-choo are on their way to the Frosty Frolic Land Train Depot.

I CAN TOUCH MY TOES (SET/2). . . In an attempt to keep fit and perhaps join in the Snowbabies Starlight Games competitions, these babies participate in some invigorating calisthentics!

I LOVE YOU THIS MUCH . . . To make sure you understand his message, this Snowbaby displays a banner to illustrate the magnitude of his feelings.

MAKE A WISH . . . Celebrating the special day with friends, this birthday baby takes a deep breath and blows out the candle (after making a wish, of course!).

MY SNOWBABY BABY DOLLS (SET/2) . . . This special pair depicts a childhood pastime and passion – playing with dolls.

PULL TOGETHER (SET/3) . . . Cooperation is essential in many activities but there always seems to be one person who just can't quite keep the rhythm!

SLIP, SLIDING AWAY ... Anticipating the exhileration of the ride, this Snowbaby is perched and waiting for a pull from a friend.

STUCK IN THE SNOW ... As the penguin waits by helplessly, this Snow baby persistently pushes a sleigh filled to the brim with wrapped goodies.

TO MY FRIEND ... Putting your feelings down on paper is often the best way to convey your gratitude to a friend.

YOU ARE MY STARSHINE ... This Snowbaby is the star of the show with the cosmic costume and its suspended satellite!

❄ Other Snowbabies Collectibles ❄

CANDLE LIGHTS (SET/6) ... A few strategically placed tapers of light are often the final touches needed to complete any display.

ICEBERGS (SET/3) ... These platforms of acrylic "icebergs" are ideal playforms for your special Snowbabies pieces.

MOON ORNAMENT HANGER ... Give your special Snowbabies miniature ornament a place of honor by hanging it on this moon display.

SNOWY PINES (SET/3) ... Evergreens never looked so good! A coating of bisque-colored snow gives them a realistic appearance.

SNOWBABIES LANDSCAPE SET (SET/7) ... This accessory set includes six white sisal trees and a bag of snow to make Frosty Frolic Land a reality!

STAR BASE ORNAMENT HANGER ... Spotlight any Snowbabies ornament with this star-designed display piece.

TOWER OF LIGHT ... Arrange your collection of Snowbabies in this fantasy-inspired ice castle complete with bisque trees and lights.

Snowbabies Friendship Club™ News

The Fun Begins . . .

In 1997, Department 56 formed its first collector's club in celebration of the Snowbabies' 10th anniversary. Since then, club members have enjoyed benefits that have included invitations to members-only breakfast events held during the 1999 International Collectible Expositions at Long Beach, California, and at Rosemont, Illinois, as well as opportunities to purchase Snowbabies items such as calendars, sweatshirts and mugs.

. . . And Continues Into The Millennium

Collectors who become members this year are in for a treat! Included in the 2000 Membership Kit is the "Sailing The Seas" welcome figurine, which depicts two nautical Snowbabies in a

unique two-piece figurine that is connected with a string. With one boat in the water and one waiting to be launched, these Snowbabies are lucky to have found this hole in the ice. Two additional pieces are included in the club kit – the "Star Bright" lapel pin and the "Celebrate Jinglebaby" ornament.

Once your application is processed by Department 56, a personalized 2000 Membership Card and Certificate will be mailed to you in addition to a one-year subscription (four issues) to the club newsletter, *Friendship News*, which provides valuable Snowbabies information, including new product introductions, retirement announcements, special events, display ideas, collector displays and opportunities to purchase special Snowbabies-related items from the Club Marketplace section.

Each renewing member will receive two gifts: a Snowbabies note pad and a package of five "Friendship Charms" to wear on your previous year's Friendship Pin. The charms are a Year 2000 gold star, a polar bear, a walrus, a snowman and a dimensional star.

Crystal Says "Goodbye"

You are also be eligible to purchase the Club exclusive piece, "Storytime," which is the final design in the series of three club pieces that feature Crystal, the little girl who discovered Frosty Frolic Land. With the purchase of this figurine, you also receive a pocket-sized booklet with excerpts from "Winter Tales of the Snowbabies," the hardcover book from Department 56.

How To Join

The yearly membership fee is $37.50, and applications for the 2000 club year will be accepted through December 31, 2000. There are several ways to join the club:

1. Purchase a membership kit or pick up an application at an authorized Snowbabies retailer in your area.

2. Call Department 56 toll-free at 1-888-SNOWBABY (766-9222) and have your credit card information available.

3. Go to the Department 56 web site (*www.department56.com*) and print out an enrollment form to mail in. You will also be able to join the club directly on-line in the near future. Check the Department 56 web site for more information or contact:

SNOWBABIES FRIENDSHIP CLUB
P. O. Box 120
South St. Paul, MN 55075-0120
1-888-SNOWBABY

Recent Retirements

T he following Snowbabies figurines, ornaments and other collectibles retired in December 1999, while the Snowbunnies listed here retired in the Spring of 1999. Included in parentheses is the date of issue and item number for each retired piece.

SNOWBABIES

Figurines

- ❏ Best Little Star (1997, #68842)
- ❏ Celebrate (Winter Celebration 1999 event piece, 1999, #68941)
- ❏ Come Fly With Me (LE-22,500, 1998, #68920)
- ❏ Five-Part Harmony (1996, #68824)
- ❏ Hold On Tight (1986, #79561)
- ❏ How Many Days 'Til Christmas? (1998, #68882)
- ❏ I See You (set/2, 1995, #68780)
- ❏ I'll Play A Christmas Tune (1995, #68801)
- ❏ Jack Frost . . . A Touch Of Winter's Magic (1994, #68543)
- ❏ Just One Little Candle (1992, #68233)
- ❏ Let's Go Skiing (1992, #68152)
- ❏ A Little Night Light (1996, #68823)
- ❏ Mush! (set/2, 1995, #68805)
- ❏ We Make A Great Pair (1993, #68438)
- ❏ Whistle While You Work (1997, #68854)
- ❏ Winter Play On A Snowy Day (set/4, 1998, #68880)
- ❏ Wish Upon A Falling Star (1997, #68839)
- ❏ You Are My Lucky Star (set/2, 1996, #68814)
- ❏ You Didn't Forget Me! (1992, #68217)

Ornaments

- ❏ Frosty Frolic Friends – 1999 (Winter Celebration 1999 event piece, #68950)
- ❏ Joy (set/3, 1995, #68807)
- ❏ Moon Beams (1987, #79510)
- ❏ Snowbaby – Mini, Winged Pair (set/2, lite-up, 1987, #79766)
- ❏ Star Bright (1989, #79901)

Pewter Miniatures

- ❏ Best Little Star (1997, #76718)
- ❏ Collector's Sign (accessory, 1989, #76201)
- ❏ Five-Part Harmony (set/2, 1996, #76710)
- ❏ I See You (set/2, 1995, #76694)
- ❏ I'm Making Snowballs! (1989, #76023)
- ❏ I'm So Sleepy (1996, #76700)
- ❏ Let's Go Skating (1994, #76643)
- ❏ Let's Go Skiing (1992, #76368)
- ❏ There's No Place Like Home (1996, #76708)

Pewter Miniatures, cont.

❏ What Shall We Do Today? (set/2, 1995, #76546)

Hinged Boxes

❏ Celebrate (1997, #68847)
❏ Hold On Tight (1998, #68884)
❏ Sweet Heart (Mother's Day 1999 event piece, 1998, #68930)

Musicals & Waterglobes

❏ Heigh-Ho (musical & waterglobe, 1997, #68872)
❏ I Love You From The Bottom Of My Heart
  (Mother's Day 1999 event piece, musical, 1998, #68921)
❏ Jingle Bell (musical & waterglobe, 1997, #68871)
❏ Moon Beams (musical & waterglobe, 1997, #68873)
❏ Once Upon A Time (musical, 1996, #68832)
❏ Sliding Through The Milky Way (musical, 1996, #68833)

Other Snowbabies Collectibles

❏ Candle Light . . . Season Bright (tree topper, 1997, #68863)
❏ Candlelight Trees (set/3, 1997, #68861)
❏ I'm The Star Atop Your Tree! (tree topper, 1997, #68862)
❏ A Little Night Light (lamp, 1996, #68836)
❏ Moonbeams (night light, 1996, #68835)
❏ Snowbaby Shelf Unit (1997, #68874)
❏ You're My Snowbaby (picture frame, 1996, #68834)

SNOWBUNNIES

Figurines

❏ Can You Come Out & Play? (LE-1999, 1998, #26309)
❏ Is There Room For Me? (1996, #26275)
❏ It's Working . . . We're Going Faster! (1995, #26190)
❏ Let's All Sing Like The Birdies Sing (set/2, 1996, #26276)
❏ My Woodland Wagon, Parked In Robins Nest
  Thicket (set/2, lighted, 1995, #26247)
❏ Slow-moving Vehicle (set/2, 1996, #26280)
❏ To Market, To Market, Delivering Eggs! (set/3, 1996, #26281)
❏ Welcome To The Neighborhood (1996, #26277)
❏ You Better Watch Out Or I'll Catch You! (1995, #26220)

Hinged Boxes

❏ Abracadabra (1997, #26298)

Musicals & Waterglobes

❏ And "B" Is For Bunny (moving musical figure, 1997, #26290)
❏ Be My Baby Bunny Bee (revolving musical, 1997, #26294)
❏ Rock-A-Bye Bunny (musical & waterglobe, 1996, #26285)
❏ You Make Me Laugh! (musical, 1996, #26284)

Snowbabies™ Top Ten

This section highlights the ten most valuable retired Snowbabies pieces as determined by their 2000 secondary market values. Each piece has top dollar value and shows a significant percentage increase in value from its original price, as shown by our Market Meter.

Frosty Frolic (LE-4,800)
Figurine • #79812
Issued 1988 • Retired 1989
Original Price: $35 • Market Value: $1,080
Market Meter: +2,986%

Snowbabies Climbing On A Tree (set/2)
Figurine • #79715
Issued 1987 • Retired 1989
Original Price: $25 • Market Value: $875
Market Meter: +3,400%

Allison & Duncan (set/2)
Papier-Maché Dolls • #77305
Issued 1988 • Retired 1989
Original Price: $200 • Market Value: $870
Market Meter: +335%

Snowbabies Riding Sleds
Waterglobe & Music Box • #79758
Issued 1987 • Retired 1988
Original Price: $40 • Market Value: $750
Market Meter: +1,775%

Mickey's New Friend
Figurine (Disney Exclusive) • #7145
Issued 1994 • Retired 1995
Original Price: $50 • Market Value: $675
Market Meter: +1,250%

Catch A Falling Star
Waterglobe & Music Box • #79677
Issued 1986 • Retired 1987
Original Price: $18 • Market Value: $645
Market Meter: +3,483%

Snowbaby Porcelain Music Box
Music Box • #79502
Issued 1986 • Retired 1987
Original Price: $27.50 • Market Value: $625
Market Meter: +2,173%

Snowbaby Holding Picture Frame (set/2)
Picture Frame • #79707
Issued 1986 • Retired 1987
Original Price: $15 • Market Value: $575
Market Meter: +3,733%

Snowbaby Standing
Waterglobe • #79642
Issued 1986 • Retired 1987
Original Price: $7.50 • Market Value: $455
Market Meter: +5,967%

Snowbaby With Wings
Waterglobe (lighted) • #79731
Issued 1987 • Retired 1988
Original Price: $20 • Market Value: $430
Market Meter: +2,050%

How To Use
Your Value Guide

2   #79847

All Fall Down (set/4)
Issued: 1989 • Retired: 1991
Original Price: $36
Market Value: $79

1. Locate your piece in the Value Guide. The Snowbabies porcelain bisque figurines are listed first, followed by Snowbabies ornaments, miniature ornaments, mercury glass ornaments, pewter miniatures, hinged boxes, musicals and waterglobes, other Snowbabies collectibles and Snowbabies Friendship Club pieces. Next are Snowbunnies figurines, hinged boxes, and musicals and waterglobes, then Easter Collectible figurines. All pieces are listed alphabetically within each section, except the Snowbabies Friendship Club pieces are listed in chronological order by club year, then in alphabetical order within each grouping. To quickly locate a piece, refer to the numerical and alphabetical indexes, beginning on page 120.

Figurines

	Price Paid	Value
1.	$36	$79
2.		
3.		
4.		
5.		
6.		
	$36	$79
Totals		

2. Find the market value of your piece. If no market value has been established, the piece is listed as "N/E." The secondary market value for current pieces is the 2000 suggested retail price.

3. Record the retail price you paid as well as the secondary market value in the corresponding boxes at the bottoms of each of the pages.

4. Calculate the total value for each page by adding all of the values in each column. Use a pencil so you can change the totals as your collection grows.

5. Transfer the totals from each page to the "Total Value of My Collection" worksheet found on page 107.

6. Add the totals together to determine the overall value of your Snowbabies collection.

Snowbabies

The Snowbabies family continues to grow and includes new pieces in The Guest Collection and the brand new *Snowbabies Starlight Games*. The line also features an assortment of ornaments, pewter miniatures, musicals, waterglobes and other Snowbabies collectibles for collectors to discover.

1 #68943

All Aboard The Star Express (set/4)
Issued: 1999 • Current
Original Price: $55
Market Value: $55

2 #79847

All Fall Down (set/4)
Issued: 1989 • Retired: 1991
Original Price: $36
Market Value: $79

3 #68860

All We Need Is Love
(Mother's Day
1997 event piece)
Issued: 1997 • Retired: 1998
Original Price: $32.50
Market Value: $36

4 #68923

. . . And That Spells BABY (set/4)
Issued: 1998 • Current
Original Price: $50
Market Value: $50

5 #79774

Are All These Mine?
Issued: 1988 • Retired: 1998
Original Price: $10
Market Value: $26

6 #68756

Are You On My List?
Issued: 1995 • Retired: 1998
Original Price: $25
Market Value: $35

Figurines	
Price Paid	Value
1.	
2.	
3.	
4.	
5.	
6.	

Totals

1 #68957

Batter Up
(Ideation early release)
Issued: 1999 • Current
Original Price: $16.50
Market Value: $16.50

2 #69047

New!

Batter Up
Starlight Games
Issued: 1999 • Current
Original Price: $16.50
Market Value: $16.50

3 #79588

Best Friends
Issued: 1986 • Retired: 1989
Original Price: $12
Market Value: $140

4 #68842

Best Little Star
Issued: 1997 • Retired: 1999
Original Price: $16
Market Value: $18

5 #68624

Bringing Starry Pines
Issued: 1994 • Retired: 1997
Original Price: $35
Market Value: $40

6 #68063

Can I Help, Too?
(LE-18,500)
Issued: 1992 • Retired: 1992
Original Price: $48
Market Value: $88

Figurines		
	Price Paid	Value
1.		
2.		
3.		
4.		
5.		
6.		
7.		
8.		
Totals		

7 #68381

Can I Open It Now?
(1993 event piece)
Issued: 1993 • Retired: 1993
Original Price: $15
Market Value: $40

8 #68941

Celebrate
(Winter Celebration
1999 event piece)
Issued: 1999 • Retired: 1999
Original Price: $60
Market Value: $62

1 #68816

Climb Every Mountain
(LE-22,500)
Issued: 1996 • Retired: 1996
Original Price: $75
Market Value: $140

2 #68920

Come Fly With Me
(LE-22,500)
Issued: 1998 • Retired: 1999
Original Price: $165
Market Value: $170

3 #69019

Come Sail With Me
Issued: 1999 • Current
Original Price: $60
Market Value: $60

4 #68349

Crossing Starry Skies
Issued: 1993 • Retired: 1997
Original Price: $35
Market Value: $40

5 #68080

Dancing To A Tune
(set/3)
Issued: 1991 • Retired: 1995
Original Price: $30
Market Value: $48

6 #79685

Don't Fall Off!
Issued: 1987 • Retired: 1990
Original Price: $12.50
Market Value: $99

7 #79600

Down The Hill We Go!
Issued: 1987 • Current
Original Price: $20
Market Value: $22.50

8 #69017

New!

**Even A Small Light
Shines In The Darkness**
Issued: 1999 • Current
Original Price: $45
Market Value: $45

Figurines	
Price Paid	Value
1.	
2.	
3.	
4.	
5.	
6.	
7.	
8.	

Totals

1 #69035

New!

Falling For You
Issued: 1999 • Current
Original Price: $18
Market Value: $18

2 #79855

Finding Fallen Stars
(LE-6,000)
Issued: 1989 • Retired: 1990
Original Price: $32.50
Market Value: $175

3 #68098

Fishing For Dreams
Issued: 1991 • Retired: 1994
Original Price: $28
Market Value: $45

4 #68824

Five-Part Harmony
Issued: 1996 • Retired: 1999
Original Price: $45
Market Value: $47

5 #68944

Follow Me (LE-2000)
Issued: 1999 • Current
Original Price: $17.50
Market Value: $17.50

6 #79812

Frosty Frolic (LE-4,800)
Issued: 1988 • Retired: 1989
Original Price: $35
Market Value: $1,080

7 #79839

Frosty Fun
Issued: 1989 • Retired: 1991
Original Price: $27.50
Market Value: $60

Figurines

	Price Paid	Value
1.		
2.		
3.		
4.		
5.		
6.		
7.		

Totals

1 #217-468

New!

A Gift For You
(Avon exclusive, Jan.)
Issued: 2000 • Current
Original Price: $9.99
Market Value: $9.99

2 #217-491

New!

A Gift For You
(Avon exclusive, Feb.)
Issued: 2000 • Current
Original Price: $9.99
Market Value: $9.99

3 #220-040

New!

A Gift For You
(Avon exclusive, March)
Issued: 2000 • Current
Original Price: $9.99
Market Value: $9.99

4 #220-403

New!

A Gift For You
(Avon exclusive, April)
Issued: 2000 • Current
Original Price: $9.99
Market Value: $9.99

5 #221-429

New!

A Gift For You
(Avon exclusive, May)
Issued: 2000 • Current
Original Price: $9.99
Market Value: $9.99

6 #221-558

New!

A Gift For You
(Avon exclusive, June)
Issued: 2000 • Current
Original Price: $9.99
Market Value: $9.99

7 #221-907

New!

A Gift For You
(Avon exclusive, July)
Issued: 2000 • Current
Original Price: $9.99
Market Value: $9.99

8 #222-129

New!

A Gift For You
(Avon exclusive, Aug.)
Issued: 2000 • Current
Original Price: $9.99
Market Value: $9.99

Figurines		
	Price Paid	Value
1.		
2.		
3.		
4.		
5.		
6.		
7.		
8.		
Totals		

1 #222-626

New!

A Gift For You
(Avon exclusive, Sept.)
Issued: 2000 • Current
Original Price: $9.99
Market Value: $9.99

2 #224-136

New!

A Gift For You
(Avon exclusive, Oct.)
Issued: 2000 • Current
Original Price: $9.99
Market Value: $9.99

3 #222-812

New!

A Gift For You
(Avon exclusive, Nov.)
Issued: 2000 • Current
Original Price: $9.99
Market Value: $9.99

4 #224-102

New!

A Gift For You
(Avon exclusive, Dec.)
Issued: 2000 • Current
Original Price: $9.99
Market Value: $9.99

5 #69901

**A Gift So Fine From
Madeline** (Mother's Day
1999 event piece)
The Guest Collection
Issued: 1998 • Current
Original Price: $50
Market Value: $50

6 #79553

Give Me A Push!
Issued: 1986 • Retired: 1990
Original Price: $12
Market Value: $80

Figurines	
Price Paid	Value
1.	
2.	
3.	
4.	
5.	
6.	
7.	
8.	

Totals

7 #68853

**Heigh-Ho, Heigh-Ho,
To Frolic Land We Go!**
Issued: 1997 • Current
Original Price: $48
Market Value: $48

8 #68179

Help Me, I'm Stuck!
Issued: 1992 • Retired: 1994
Original Price: $32.50
Market Value: $50

1 #79820

Helpful Friends
Issued: 1989 • Retired: 1993
Original Price: $30
Market Value: $52

2 #69005

New!

Hit The Mark
Starlight Games
Issued: 1999 • Current
Original Price: $25
Market Value: $25

3 #79561

Hold On Tight!
Issued: 1986 • Retired: 1999
Original Price: $12
Market Value: $24

4 #68882

How Many Days 'Til Christmas?
Issued: 1998 • Retired: 1999
Original Price: $36
Market Value: $40

5 #68927

I Can Touch My Toes
(set/2)
Issued: 1998 • Current
Original Price: $30
Market Value: $30

6 #68800

I Can't Find Him!
Issued: 1995 • Retired: 1998
Original Price: $37.50
Market Value: $45

7 #68942

I Caribou You
Issued: 1999 • Current
Original Price: $50
Market Value: $50

8 #68748

I Found The Biggest Star Of All!
Issued: 1995 • Retired: 1998
Original Price: $16
Market Value: $19

Figurines

	Price Paid	Value
1.		
2.		
3.		
4.		
5.		
6.		
7.		
8.		

Totals

Value Guide – Department 56® Snowbabies™

Snowbabies™

1   #68365

I Found Your Mittens!
(set/2)
Issued: 1993 • Retired: 1996
Original Price: $30
Market Value: $43

2   #69900

I Have A Feeling We're Not In Kansas Anymore
(Winter Celebration 1998 event piece)
The Guest Collection
Issued: 1998 • Current
Original Price: $50
Market Value: $50

3   #68918

I Love You This Much!
Issued: 1998 • Current
Original Price: $16.50
Market Value: $16.50

4   #68020

I Made This Just For You!
Issued: 1991 • Retired: 1998
Original Price: $15
Market Value: $22

5   #68136

I Need A Hug
Issued: 1992 • Current
Original Price: $20
Market Value: $20

6   #68780

I See You! (set/2)
Issued: 1995 • Retired: 1999
Original Price: $27.50
Market Value: $31

7   #25430224

I'll Light The Way
(Disney exclusive)
Issued: 1999 • Current
Original Price: $27.50
Market Value: $27.50

8   #69009

New!

I'll Love You Always
(Spring Promotion 2000 event piece)
Issued: 1999 • Current
Original Price: $30
Market Value: $30

Figurines

	Price Paid	Value
1.		
2.		
3.		
4.		
5.		
6.		
7.		
8.		

Totals

36

1 #68801

I'll Play A Christmas Tune
Issued: 1995 • Retired: 1999
Original Price: $16
Market Value: $20

2 #68004

I'll Put Up The Tree!
Issued: 1991 • Retired: 1995
Original Price: $24
Market Value: $37

3 #68357

I'll Teach You A Trick
Issued: 1993 • Retired: 1996
Original Price: $24
Market Value: $36

4 #68420

I'm Making An Ice Sculpture!
Issued: 1993 • Retired: 1996
Original Price: $30
Market Value: $46

5 #79626

I'm Making Snowballs!
Issued: 1986 • Retired: 1992
Original Price: $12
Market Value: $41

6 #68527

I'm Right Behind You!
Issued: 1994 • Retired: 1997
Original Price: $60
Market Value: $66

7 #68810

I'm So Sleepy
Issued: 1996 • Current
Original Price: $16
Market Value: $16

8 #68039

Is That For Me? (set/2)
Issued: 1991 • Retired: 1993
Original Price: $32.50
Market Value: $55

Figurines

	Price Paid	Value
1.		
2.		
3.		
4.		
5.		
6.		
7.		
8.		

Totals

Snowbabies™

1 #68822

It's A Grand Old Flag
(set/3, w/Snowbabies flag and one of eight national
flags from Canada, France, Germany, Italy, Japan,
The Netherlands, United Kingdom or United States)
Issued: 1996 • Retired: 1998
Original Price: $25
Market Values: w/U.S. flag $35
w/Canadian flag $45 – w/any other flag $50

2 #68821

It's Snowing!
Issued: 1996 • Current
Original Price: $16.50
Market Value: $16.50

3 #68811

**Jack Frost . . .
A Sleighride Through
The Stars** (set/3)
Issued: 1996 • Current
Original Price: $110
Market Value: $110

4 #68543

**Jack Frost . . . A Touch
Of Winter's Magic**
Issued: 1994 • Retired: 1999
Original Price: $90
Market Value: $110

5 #69020

New!

**Jack Frost . . . Through
The Frosty Forest**
Issued: 1999 • Current
Original Price: $150
Market Value: $150

Figurines	
Price Paid	Value
1.	
2.	
3.	
4.	
5.	
6.	
7.	
Totals	

6 #68855

Jingle Bell
Issued: 1997 • Current
Original Price: $16
Market Value: $16

7 #68241

Join The Parade
Issued: 1992 • Retired: 1994
Original Price: $37.50
Market Value: $55

1   #69021

New!

**Jolly Friends
Forevermore (set/11)**
Issued: 1999 • Current
Original Price: $50
Market Value: $50

2   #68881

**A Journey For Two
By Caribou!**
Issued: 1998 • Current
Original Price: $50
Market Value: $50

3   #69036

New!

Jumping For Joy
Issued: 1999 • Current
Original Price: $18
Market Value: $18

4   #68233

Just One Little Candle
Issued: 1992 • Retired: 1999
Original Price: $15
Market Value: $18

5   #69902

**A Kiss For You And
2000 Too**
(Winter Celebration
1999 event piece)
The Guest Collection
Issued: 1999 • Current
Original Price: $50
Market Value: $50

6   #68454

Let's All Chime In!
(set/2)
Issued: 1993 • Retired: 1995
Original Price: $37.50
Market Value: $56

7   #6850

Let's Be Friends
(Disney exclusive)
Issued: 1998 • Retired: 1999
Original Price: $25
Market Value: $265

8   #68850

Let's Go See Jack Frost
(10th Anniversary
1997 event piece)
Issued: 1997 • Retired: 1997
Original Price: $60
Market Value: $85

Figurines	Price Paid	Value
1.		
2.		
3.		
4.		
5.		
6.		
7.		
8.		
Totals		

Value Guide – Department 56® Snowbabies™

1 #68608

Let's Go Skating
Issued: 1994 • Retired: 1998
Original Price: $16.50
Market Value: $19

2 #68152

Let's Go Skiing
Issued: 1992 • Retired: 1999
Original Price: $15
Market Value: $23

3 #68632

**Lift Me Higher,
I Can't Reach!**
Issued: 1994 • Retired: 1998
Original Price: $75
Market Value: N/E

4 #68823

A Little Night Light
Issued: 1996 • Retired: 1999
Original Price: $32.50
Market Value: $36

5 #69011

New!

The Littlest Angel
Issued: 1999 • Current
Original Price: $18
Market Value: $18

6 #68195

Look What I Can Do!
Issued: 1992 • Retired: 1996
Original Price: $16.50
Market Value: $32

Figurines

	Price Paid	Value
1.		
2.		
3.		
4.		
5.		
6.		
7.		
Totals		

7 #68330

Look What I Found!
Issued: 1993 • Retired: 1997
Original Price: $45
Market Value: $55

Value Guide — Department 56® Snowbabies™

1 #68926

Make A Wish
Issued: 1998 • Current
Original Price: $30
Market Value: $30

2 #7145

Mickey's New Friend
(Disney exclusive)
Issued: 1994 • Retired: 1995
Original Price: $50
Market Value: $675

3 #68805

Mush! (set/2)
Issued: 1995 • Retired: 1999
Original Price: $48
Market Value: $52

4 #69016

**Music From
The Highest (set/3)**
Issued: 1999 • Current
Original Price: $45
Market Value: $45

5 #68919

**My Snowbaby
Baby Dolls (set/2)**
Issued: 1998 • Current
Original Price: $32.50
Market Value: $32.50

6 #68390

**Now I Lay Me Down
To Sleep**
Issued: 1993 • Current
Original Price: $13.50
Market Value: $13.50

7 #6859

Off To A Good Start
(Bachman's exclusive)
Issued: 1999 • Current
Original Price: $32.50
Market Value: $32.50

8 #68858

**One For You,
One For Me**
Issued: 1997 • Current
Original Price: $27.50
Market Value: $27.50

Figurines

	Price Paid	Value
1.		
2.		
3.		
4.		
5.		
6.		
7.		
8.		

Totals

Snowbabies™

1 #69004

New!

Over The Top
Starlight Games
Issued: 1999 • Current
Original Price: $25
Market Value: $25

2 #68804

Parade Of Penguins
(set/6)
Issued: 1995 • Current
Original Price: $15
Market Value: $15

3 #79863

Penguin Parade
Issued: 1989 • Retired: 1992
Original Price: $25
Market Value: $53

4 #79472

Playing Games Is Fun!
Issued: 1990 • Retired: 1993
Original Price: $30
Market Value: $52

5 #79782

Polar Express
Issued: 1988 • Retired: 1992
Original Price: $22
Market Value: $97

6 #68924

Pull Together
Issued: 1998 • Current
Original Price: $60
Market Value: $60

Figurines

	Price Paid	Value
1.		
2.		
3.		
4.		
5.		
6.		
7.		
8.		

Totals

7 #254-927

Reach For The Moon
(Avon exclusive)
Issued: 1999 • Current
Original Price: $19.99
Market Value: $19.99

8 #79456

Read Me A Story!
Issued: 1990 • Current
Original Price: $25
Market Value: $25

Value Guide – Department 56® Snowbabies™

1 #68764

**Ring The Bells . . .
It's Christmas!**
Issued: 1995 • Current
Original Price: $40
Market Value: $40

2 #69007

New!

Score
Starlight Games
Issued: 1999 • Current
Original Price: $16.50
Market Value: $16.50

3 #69013

New!

Shake It Up, Baby
Issued: 1999 • Current
Original Price: $20
Market Value: $20

4 #68209

Shall I Play For You?
Issued: 1992 • Retired: 1998
Original Price: $16.50
Market Value: $23

5 #68859

Ship O' Dreams (set/2)
Issued: 1997 • Current
Original Price: $135
Market Value: $135

6 #6808

**Slip, Sliding Away
(early release to
selected retailers)**
Issued: 1998 • Retired: 1998
Original Price: $30
Market Value: N/E

7 #68934

Slip, Sliding Away
Issued: 1998 • Current
Original Price: $28
Market Value: $28

8 #79715

**Snowbabies Climbing
On Tree (set/2)**
Issued: 1987 • Retired: 1989
Original Price: $25
Market Value: $875

Figurines		
	Price Paid	Value
1.		
2.		
3.		
4.		
5.		
6.		
7.		
8.		
Totals		

43

Value Guide — Department 56® Snowbabies™

1 #68373

So Much Work To Do!
Issued: 1993 • Retired: 1998
Original Price: $18
Market Value: $29

2 #68403

Somewhere In Dreamland
(one star bottomstamp added each year available)
Issued: 1993 • Retired: 1997
Original Price: $85
Market Value: $100

3 #79480

A Special Delivery
Issued: 1990 • Retired: 1994
Original Price: $13.50
Market Value: $29

4 #68803

A Star-In-The-Box
(exclusive to selected retailers)
Issued: 1995 • Retired: 1996
Original Price: $18
Market Value: $48

5 #68925

Stargazer's Castle
Issued: 1998 • Current
Original Price: $40
Market Value: $40

6 #68817

Stargazing
(set/9, early release as #7800 to selected retailers)
Issued: 1996 • Retired: 1998
Original Price: $40
Market Value: $42

Figurines

	Price Paid	Value
1.		
2.		
3.		
4.		
5.		
6.		
7.		
8.		
Totals		

7 #68856

Starlight Serenade
Issued: 1997 • Current
Original Price: $25
Market Value: $25

8 #69015

New!

Starlight, Starbright
Issued: 1999 • Current
Original Price: $25
Market Value: $25

Value Guide – Department 56® Snowbabies™

1 #68225

Stars In-A-Row, Tic-Tac-Toe
Issued: 1992 • Retired: 1995
Original Price: $32.50
Market Value: $45

2 #68616

Stringing Fallen Stars
Issued: 1994 • Retired: 1998
Original Price: $25
Market Value: $27

3 #6806

Stuck In The Snow
(early release to selected retailers)
Issued: 1998 • Retired: 1998
Original Price: $30
Market Value: N/E

4 #68932

Stuck In The Snow
Issued: 1998 • Current
Original Price: $30
Market Value: $30

5 #68857

Thank You
Issued: 1997 • Current
Original Price: $32.50
Market Value: $32.50

6 #68535

There's Another One!
Issued: 1994 • Retired: 1998
Original Price: $24
Market Value: $27

7 #68820

There's No Place Like Home
Issued: 1996 • Current
Original Price: $16.50
Market Value: $16.50

8 #69010

New!

They're Coming From Oz, Oh My!
The Guest Collection
Issued: 1999 • Current
Original Price: $55
Market Value: $55

Figurines	
Price Paid	Value
1.	
2.	
3.	
4.	
5.	
6.	
7.	
8.	

Totals

45

1 #68055

This Is Where We Live!
Issued: 1991 • Retired: 1994
Original Price: $60
Market Value: $80

2 #68160

This Will Cheer You Up
Issued: 1992 • Retired: 1994
Original Price: $30
Market Value: $52

3 #68888

Three Tiny Trumpeters
(set/2, Winter Celebration
1998 event piece,
available with all gold,
all silver or combination)
Issued: 1998 • Retired: 1998
Original Price: $50
Market Value: $58

4 #79790

Tiny Trio (set/3)
Issued: 1988 • Retired: 1990
Original Price: $20
Market Value: $184

5 #68917

To My Friend
Issued: 1998 • Current
Original Price: $18
Market Value: $18

6 #79570

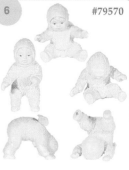

Tumbling In The Snow!
(set/5)
Issued: 1987 • Retired: 1993
Original Price: $35
Market Value: $95

Figurines

	Price Paid	Value
1.		
2.		
3.		
4.		
5.		
6.		
7.		
Totals		

7 #79421

Twinkle Little Stars
(set/2)
Issued: 1990 • Retired: 1993
Original Price: $37.50
Market Value: $60

Value Guide — Department 56® Snowbabies™

1 #68840

Two Little Babies On The Go!
Issued: 1997 • Current
Original Price: $32.50
Market Value: $32.50

2 #68128

Wait For Me!
Issued: 1992 • Retired: 1994
Original Price: $48
Market Value: $64

3 #68071

Waiting For Christmas
Issued: 1991 • Retired: 1993
Original Price: $27.50
Market Value: $50

4 #68438

We Make A Great Pair
Issued: 1993 • Retired: 1999
Original Price: $30
Market Value: $34

5 #79464

We Will Make It Shine!
Issued: 1990 • Retired: 1992
Original Price: $45
Market Value: $77

6 #68659

We'll Plant The Starry Pines (set/2)
Issued: 1994 • Retired: 1997
Original Price: $37.50
Market Value: $43

7 #68802

We're Building An Icy Igloo
Issued: 1995 • Retired: 1998
Original Price: $70
Market Value: N/E

8 #68772

What Shall We Do Today?
Issued: 1995 • Retired: 1997
Original Price: $32.50
Market Value: $38

Figurines	
Price Paid	Value
1.	
2.	
3.	
4.	
5.	
6.	
7.	
8.	
Totals	

Snowbabies™

1 #68819

When The Bough Breaks
Issued: 1996 • Current
Original Price: $30
Market Value: $30

2 #68411

Where Did He Go?
Issued: 1993 • Current
Original Price: $35
Market Value: $35

3 #68560

Where Did You Come From?
Issued: 1994 • Retired: 1997
Original Price: $40
Market Value: $55

4 #68812

Which Way's Up?
Issued: 1996 • Retired: 1997
Original Price: $30
Market Value: $35

5 #68854

Whistle While You Work
Issued: 1997 • Retired: 1999
Original Price: $32.50
Market Value: $36

6 #79499

Who Are You?
(LE-12,500)
Issued: 1990 • Retired: 1991
Original Price: $32.50
Market Value: $135

Figurines

	Price Paid	Value
1.		
2.		
3.		
4.		
5.		
6.		
7.		
8.		

Totals

7 #68012

Why Don't You Talk To Me?
Issued: 1991 • Current
Original Price: $24
Market Value: $24

8 #68446

Will It Snow Today?
Issued: 1993 • Retired: 1995
Original Price: $45
Market Value: $67

Value Guide – Department 56® Snowbabies™

1   #68144

Winken, Blinken & Nod
Issued: 1992 • Retired: 1998
Original Price: $60
Market Value: $69

2   #68880

**Winter Play On
A Snowy Day (set/4)**
Issued: 1998 • Retired: 1999
Original Price: $48
Market Value: $52

3   #79740

Winter Surprise!
Issued: 1987 • Retired: 1992
Original Price: $15
Market Value: $41

4   #68839

**Wish Upon
A Falling Star**
Issued: 1997 • Retired: 1999
Original Price: $75
Market Value: $79

5   #79430

Wishing On A Star
Issued: 1990 • Retired: 1994
Original Price: $20
Market Value: $44

6   #68843

**Wishing You
A Merry Christmas!**
Issued: 1997 • Retired: 1998
Original Price: $40
Market Value: $45

7   #68813

**With Hugs & Kisses
(set/2)**
Issued: 1996 • Retired: 1998
Original Price: $32.50
Market Value: $35

8   #68814

**You Are My Lucky Star
(set/2)**
Issued: 1996 • Retired: 1999
Original Price: $35
Market Value: $39

Figurines	
Price Paid	Value
1.	
2.	
3.	
4.	
5.	
6.	
7.	
8.	

Totals   49

1 #68945

You Are My Starshine
Issued: 1999 • Current
Original Price: $17.50
Market Value: $17.50

2 #68187

You Can't Find Me!
Issued: 1992 • Retired: 1996
Original Price: $45
Market Value: $57

3 #68217

You Didn't Forget Me!
Issued: 1992 • Retired: 1999
Original Price: $32.50
Market Value: $40

4 #68818

You Need Wings Too!
Issued: 1996 • Current
Original Price: $25
Market Value: $25

5 #6809

**You've Got The Cutest
Little Baby Face**
(early release to
selected retailers)
Issued: 1998 • Retired: 1998
Original Price: $32.50
Market Value: N/E

6 #68933

**You've Got The Cutest
Little Baby Face**
Issued: 1998 • Current
Original Price: $32.50
Market Value: $32.50

Figurines

	Price Paid	Value
1.		
2.		
3.		
4.		
5.		
6.		

Ornaments

7.		

Totals

Ornaments

7 #68828

Baby's 1st Rattle
Issued: 1996 • Retired: 1998
Original Price: $15
Market Value: $22

1 #68913

Baby's First Photo
Issued: 1998 • Current
Original Price: $8.50
Market Value: $8.50

2 #68667

Be My Baby
Issued: 1994 • Retired: 1998
Original Price: $15
Market Value: $20

3 #6861

Believe 2000
(1999-2000 signing
event gift)
Issued: 1999 • Current
Original Price: N/A
Market Value: N/A

4 #68864

**Candle Light . . .
Season Bright**
Issued: 1997 • Current
Original Price: $13.50
Market Value: $13.50

5 #68586

First Star Jinglebaby
Issued: 1994 • Retired: 1997
Original Price: $10
Market Value: $14

6 #68865

**Five, Six,
A Drum With Sticks**
Issued: 1997 • Current
Original Price: $13.50
Market Value: $13.50

7 #68885

Fly Me To The Moon
Issued: 1998 • Current
Original Price: $16.50
Market Value: $16.50

8 #68879

Frosty Frolic Friends
(Winter Celebration
1998 event piece)
Issued: 1998 • Retired: 1998
Original Price: $15
Market Value: $20

Ornaments

	Price Paid	Value
1.		
2.		
3.		
4.		
5.		
6.		
7.		
8.		
Totals		

1   #68950

**Frosty Frolic Friends –
1999** (Winter Celebration
1999 event piece)
Issued: 1999 • Retired: 1999
Original Price: $15
Market Value: N/E

2   #68551

**Gathering Stars
In The Sky**
Issued: 1994 • Retired: 1997
Original Price: $12.50
Market Value: $18

3   #68250

Icicle With Star (set/4)
Issued: 1992 • Retired: 1995
Original Price: $16
Market Value: $24

4   #68826

Jinglebell Jinglebaby
Issued: 1996 • Retired: 1998
Original Price: $11
Market Value: $14

5   #68807

Joy (set/3)
Issued: 1995 • Retired: 1999
Original Price: $32.50
Market Value: $35

6   #68829

Joy To The World (set/2)
Issued: 1996 • Retired: 1998
Original Price: $16.50
Market Value: $18

Ornaments

	Price Paid	Value
1.		
2.		
3.		
4.		
5.		
6.		
7.		
Totals		

7   #68675

**Juggling Stars
In The Sky**
Issued: 1994 • Retired: 1998
Original Price: $15
Market Value: $17

1 #68691

Just For You Jinglebaby
Issued: 1994 • Retired: 1998
Original Price: $11
Market Value: $15

2 #68594

**Little Drummer
Jinglebaby**
Issued: 1994 • Retired: 1997
Original Price: $10
Market Value: $14

3 #79510

Moon Beams
Issued: 1987 • Retired: 1999
Original Price: $7.50
Market Value: $11

4 #69032

New!

**Moondreams &
Hangin' On (set/2)**
Issued: 1999 • Current
Original Price: $15
Market Value: $15

5 #68110

My First Star
Issued: 1991 • Retired: 1998
Original Price: $7
Market Value: $14

6 #68900

**Nine, Ten,
You're My Best Friend**
Issued: 1998 • Current
Original Price: $12.50
Market Value: $12.50

7 #79880

Noel
Issued: 1989 • Retired: 1998
Original Price: $7.50
Market Value: $14

8 #68806

**One Little
Candle Jinglebaby**
Issued: 1995 • Retired: 1998
Original Price: $11
Market Value: $14

Ornaments	
Price Paid	Value
1.	
2.	
3.	
4.	
5.	
6.	
7.	
8.	

Totals

1 #68844

**One, Two,
High Button Shoe**
Issued: 1997 • Current
Original Price: $12.50
Market Value: $12.50

2 #7595

Overnight Delivery
(Collector's Month
1995 event piece)
Issued: 1995 • Retired: 1995
Original Price: $10
Market Value: $44

3 #68808

Overnight Delivery
Issued: 1995 • Current
Original Price: $10
Market Value: $10

4 #68914

Reach For The Moon
(set/2)
Issued: 1998 • Current
Original Price: $15
Market Value: $15

5 #79391

Rock-A-Bye Baby
Issued: 1990 • Retired: 1995
Original Price: $7
Market Value: $21

6 #68951

Royal Bootiebaby
Issued: 1999 • Current
Original Price: $13.50
Market Value: $13.50

Ornaments

Price Paid	Value
1.	
2.	
3.	
4.	
5.	
6.	
7.	
8.	

Totals

7 #68886

**Seven, Eight,
Time To Skate**
Issued: 1998 • Current
Original Price: $12.50
Market Value: $12.50

8 #79405

Snowbabies Penguin
(lite-up)
Issued: 1990 • Retired: 1992
Original Price: $5
Market Value: $29

Value Guide — Department 56® Snowbabies™

1 #79413

Snowbabies Polar Bear
(lite-up)
Issued: 1990 • Retired: 1992
Original Price: $5
Market Value: $26

2 #79693

Snowbaby Adrift
(lite-up)
Issued: 1987 • Retired: 1990
Original Price: $8.50
Market Value: $133

3 #79537

Snowbaby Crawling
(lite-up)
Issued: 1986 • Retired: 1992
Original Price: $7
Market Value: $27

4 #68827

**Snowbaby In
My Stocking**
Issued: 1996 • Current
Original Price: $10
Market Value: $10

5 #79766

**Snowbaby - Mini,
Winged Pair**
(set/2, lite-up)
Issued: 1987 • Retired: 1999
Original Price: $9
Market Value: $12

6 #79618

**Snowbaby On
A Brass Ribbon**
Issued: 1986 • Retired: 1989
Original Price: $8
Market Value: $170

7 #79529

Snowbaby Sitting
(lite-up)
Issued: 1986 • Retired: 1990
Original Price: $7
Market Value: $46

8 #79545

Snowbaby Winged
(lite-up)
Issued: 1986 • Retired: 1990
Original Price: $7
Market Value: $60

Ornaments

	Price Paid	Value
1.		
2.		
3.		
4.		
5.		
6.		
7.		
8.		

Totals

1   #68489

Sprinkling Stars In The Sky
Issued: 1993 • Retired: 1997
Original Price: $12.50
Market Value: $16

2   #79901

Star Bright
Issued: 1989 • Retired: 1999
Original Price: $7.50
Market Value: $11

3   #68825

Starry Pine Jinglebaby
Issued: 1996 • Retired: 1998
Original Price: $11
Market Value: $20

4   #68306

Starry, Starry Night
Issued: 1992 • Current
Original Price: $12.50
Market Value: $12.50

5   #68683

Stars In My Stocking Jinglebaby
Issued: 1994 • Retired: 1998
Original Price: $11
Market Value: $13

6   #79898

Surprise!
Issued: 1989 • Retired: 1994
Original Price: $12
Market Value: $30

7   #68101

Swinging On A Star
Issued: 1991 • Current
Original Price: $9.50
Market Value: $10

Ornaments

	Price Paid	Value
1.		
2.		
3.		
4.		
5.		
6.		
7.		
Totals		

1 #68845

**Three, Four, No Room
For One More**
Issued: 1997 • Current
Original Price: $12.50
Market Value: $12.50

2 #79804

Twinkle Little Star
Issued: 1988 • Retired: 1990
Original Price: $7
Market Value: $95

3 #68470

Wee . . . This Is Fun!
Issued: 1993 • Retired: 1997
Original Price: $13.50
Market Value: $16

Miniature
Ornaments

4 #69038

New!

Best Friends
Issued: 1999 • Current
Original Price: $12.50
Market Value: $12.50

5 #68902

Celebrate
Issued: 1998 • Current
Original Price: $12.50
Market Value: $12.50

6 #68910

7 #68905

Give Me A Push
Issued: 1998 • Current
Original Price: $12.50
Market Value: $12.50

Give Someone A Hug
Issued: 1998 • Current
Original Price: $12.50
Market Value: $12.50

Ornaments		
	Price Paid	Value
1.		
2.		
3.		
Miniature Ornaments		
4.		
5.		
6.		
7.		
Totals		

57

1 #68901

I Love You
Issued: 1998 • Current
Original Price: $12.50
Market Value: $12.50

2 #68907

I'll Read You A Story
Issued: 1998 • Current
Original Price: $12.50
Market Value: $12.50

3 #68912

Let It Snow
Issued: 1998 • Current
Original Price: $12.50
Market Value: $12.50

4 #68911

Let's Go Skiing
Issued: 1998 • Current
Original Price: $12.50
Market Value: $12.50

5 #68909

My Gift To You
Issued: 1998 • Current
Original Price: $12.50
Market Value: $12.50

6 #68908

Rock-A-Bye-Baby
Issued: 1998 • Current
Original Price: $12.50
Market Value: $12.50

Miniature Ornaments

	Price Paid	Value
1.		
2.		
3.		
4.		
5.		
6.		
7.		

Totals

7 #68904

Shall I Play For You?
Issued: 1998 • Current
Original Price: $12.50
Market Value: $12.50

1 #68906

Starlight Serenade
Issued: 1998 • Current
Original Price: $12.50
Market Value: $12.50

2 #68903

Sweet Dreams
Issued: 1998 • Current
Original Price: $12.50
Market Value: $12.50

3 #69037

New!

They Call Me Joyful
Issued: 1999 • Current
Original Price: $12.50
Market Value: $12.50

Mercury Glass Ornaments

4 #68997

Snowbaby Angel
Issued: 1997 • Retired: 1998
Original Price: $18
Market Value: N/E

5 #68983

Snowbaby Drummer
Issued: 1996 • Retired: 1998
Original Price: $18
Market Value: N/E

6 #68996

Snowbaby In Skate
Issued: 1997 • Retired: 1998
Original Price: $20
Market Value: N/E

7 #68994

Snowbaby In Stocking
Issued: 1997 • Retired: 1998
Original Price: $20
Market Value: N/E

Miniature Ornaments

	Price Paid	Value
1.		
2.		
3.		

Mercury Glass Ornaments

4.		
5.		
6.		
7.		

Totals

1 #68986

Snowbaby In Package
Issued: 1996 • Retired: 1998
Original Price: $18
Market Value: N/E

2 #68998

Snowbaby Jack Frost
Issued: 1997 • Retired: 1998
Original Price: $37.50
Market Value: N/E

3 #68989

Snowbaby Jinglebaby
Issued: 1996 • Retired: 1998
Original Price: $20
Market Value: N/E

4 #68993

Snowbaby On Drum
Issued: 1997 • Retired: 1998
Original Price: $22.50
Market Value: N/E

5 #68988

Snowbaby On Moon
Issued: 1996 • Retired: 1998
Original Price: $18
Market Value: N/E

6 #68981

Snowbaby On Package
Issued: 1996 • Retired: 1998
Original Price: $18
Market Value: N/E

7 #68995

Snowbaby On Skis
Issued: 1997 • Retired: 1998
Original Price: $20
Market Value: N/E

8 #68984

Snowbaby On Snowball
Issued: 1996 • Retired: 1998
Original Price: $20
Market Value: N/E

Mercury Glass Ornaments

	Price Paid	Value
1.		
2.		
3.		
4.		
5.		
6.		
7.		
8.		
Totals		

Value Guide – Department 56® Snowbabies™

1 #68992

Snowbaby On Tree
Issued: 1997 • Retired: 1998
Original Price: $22.50
Market Value: N/E

2 #68982

Snowbaby Soldier
Issued: 1996 • Retired: 1998
Original Price: $18
Market Value: N/E

3 #68987

Snowbaby With Bell
Issued: 1996 • Retired: 1998
Original Price: $18
Market Value: N/E

4 #68990

Snowbaby With Sisal Tree
Issued: 1996 • Retired: 1998
Original Price: $20
Market Value: N/E

5 #68991

Snowbaby With Star
Issued: 1996 • Retired: 1998
Original Price: $18
Market Value: N/E

6 #68980

Snowbaby With Wreath
Issued: 1996 • Retired: 1998
Original Price: $18
Market Value: N/E

Pewter Miniatures

7 #76739

All Aboard The Star Express (set/4)
Issued: 1999 • Current
Original Price: $25
Market Value: $25

Mercury Glass Ornaments		
	Price Paid	Value
1.		
2.		
3.		
4.		
5.		
6.		
Pewter Miniatures		
7.		
Totals		

Snowbabies™

61

#76171

All Fall Down (set/4)
Issued: 1989 • Retired: 1993
Original Price: $25
Market Value: $43

#76722

All We Need Is Love
(set/3)
Issued: 1998 • Current
Original Price: $20
Market Value: $20

#76058

Are All These Mine?
Issued: 1989 • Retired: 1992
Original Price: $7
Market Value: $22

#76691

Are You On My List?
(set/2)
Issued: 1995 • Retired: 1997
Original Price: $9
Market Value: $14

#76723

Baby, It's Cold Outside
(set/2)
Issued: 1998 • Current
Original Price: $8.50
Market Value: $8.50

#76040

Best Friends
Issued: 1989 • Retired: 1994
Original Price: $10
Market Value: $23

Pewter Miniatures

	Price Paid	Value
1.		
2.		
3.		
4.		
5.		
6.		
7.		
8.		
Totals		

#76718

Best Little Star
Issued: 1997 • Retired: 1999
Original Price: $6.50
Market Value: $10

#76660

Bringing Starry Pines
(set/2)
Issued: 1994 • Retired: 1997
Original Price: $18
Market Value: $20

Value Guide — Department 56® Snowbabies™

1 #76702

Climb Every Mountain
(set/5)
Issued: 1996 • Current
Original Price: $27.50
Market Value: $27.50

2 #76201

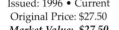

Collector's Sign
(accessory)
Issued: 1989 • Retired: 1999
Original Price: $7
Market Value: $11

3 #76309

Dancing To A Tune
(set/3)
Issued: 1991 • Retired: 1993
Original Price: $18
Market Value: $35

4 #76031

Don't Fall Off!
Issued: 1989 • Retired: 1994
Original Price: $7
Market Value: $20

5 #76066

Down The Hill We Go!
(set/2)
Issued: 1989 • Current
Original Price: $13.50
Market Value: $13.50

6 #76180

Finding Fallen Stars
(set/2)
Issued: 1989 • Retired: 1992
Original Price: $12.50
Market Value: $34

7 #76710

Five-Part Harmony
(set/2)
Issued: 1996 • Retired: 1999
Original Price: $22
Market Value: $26

8 #76120

Frosty Forest
(set/2, accessory)
Issued: 1989 • Current
Original Price: $12
Market Value: $12

Pewter Miniatures

	Price Paid	Value
1.		
2.		
3.		
4.		
5.		
6.		
7.		
8.		

Totals

1   #76139

Frosty Frolic (set/4)
Issued: 1989 • Retired: 1993
Original Price: $24
Market Value: $36

2   #76729

Frosty Frolic Ice Palace
(accessory)
Issued: 1998 • Current
Original Price: $95
Market Value: $95

3   #76198

Frosty Frolic Land
(set/3, accessory)
Issued: 1989 • Retired: 1998
Original Price: $96
Market Value: $90

4   #76112

Frosty Fun (set/2)
Issued: 1989 • Retired: 1997
Original Price: $13.50
Market Value: $16

5   #76015

Give Me A Push!
Issued: 1989 • Retired: 1994
Original Price: $7
Market Value: $22

6   #76711

Heigh-Ho, Heigh-Ho, To
Frolic Land We Go!
Issued: 1997 • Current
Original Price: $22.50
Market Value: $22.50

Pewter Miniatures

	Price Paid	Value
1.		
2.		
3.		
4.		
5.		
6.		
7.		
8.		

Totals

7   #76384

Help Me, I'm Stuck!
(set/2)
Issued: 1992 • Retired: 1997
Original Price: $15
Market Value: $18

8   #76082

Helpful Friends (set/4)
Issued: 1989 • Retired: 1992
Original Price: $13.50
Market Value: $32

Value Guide – Department 56® Snowbabies™

1 #76007

Hold On Tight!
Issued: 1989 • Retired: 1998
Original Price: $7
Market Value: $16

2 #76721

**How Many Days
'Til Christmas?**
Issued: 1998 • Current
Original Price: $18
Market Value: $18

3 #76731

New!

I Can Touch My Toes
(set/2)
Issued: 1999 • Current
Original Price: $13.50
Market Value: $13.50

4 #76695

I Can't Find Him!
(set/3)
Issued: 1995 • Retired: 1998
Original Price: $18
Market Value: $20

5 #76690

**I Found The Biggest
Star Of All**
Issued: 1995 • Retired: 1998
Original Price: $7
Market Value: $10

6 #76735

New!

I Love You This Much
Issued: 1999 • Current
Original Price: $7
Market Value: $7

7 #76287

**I Made This
Just For You!**
Issued: 1991 • Retired: 1994
Original Price: $7
Market Value: $23

8 #76406

I Need A Hug
Issued: 1992 • Retired: 1997
Original Price: $10
Market Value: $17

Pewter Miniatures

	Price Paid	Value
1.		
2.		
3.		
4.		
5.		
6.		
7.		
8.		

Totals

Value Guide – Department 56® Snowbabies™

1 #76694

I See You! (set/2)
Issued: 1995 • Retired: 1999
Original Price: $13.50
Market Value: $15

2 #76696

**I'll Play
A Christmas Tune**
Issued: 1995 • Retired: 1998
Original Price: $7.50
Market Value: $12

3 #76279

I'll Put Up The Tree!
Issued: 1991 • Retired: 1996
Original Price: $9
Market Value: $20

4 #76023

I'm Making Snowballs!
Issued: 1989 • Retired: 1999
Original Price: $7
Market Value: $7

5 #76627

**I'm Right Behind You
(set/5)**
Issued: 1994 • Retired: 1997
Original Price: $27.50
Market Value: $33

6 #76700

I'm So Sleepy
Issued: 1996 • Retired: 1999
Original Price: $7
Market Value: $9

Pewter Miniatures

	Price Paid	Value
1.		
2.		
3.		
4.		
5.		
6.		
7.		
8.		
Totals		

7 #76104

Icy Igloo
(set/2, accessory w/tree)
Issued: 1989 • Retired: 1992
Original Price: $7.50
Market Value: $28

8 #76317

Is That For Me? (set/2)
Issued: 1991 • Retired: 1993
Original Price: $12.50
Market Value: $26

1 #76705

It's A Grand Old Flag
(set/2)
Issued: 1996 • Retired: 1998
Original Price: $11
Market Value: $13

2 #76706

It's Snowing!
Issued: 1996 • Current
Original Price: $7
Market Value: $7

3 #76716

Jack Frost . . . A Touch Of Winter's Magic
(set/3)
Issued: 1997 • Current
Original Price: $27.50
Market Value: $27.50

4 #76713

Jingle Bell
Issued: 1997 • Current
Original Price: $7
Market Value: $7

5 #76457

Join The Parade (set/4)
Issued: 1992 • Retired: 1995
Original Price: $22.50
Market Value: $30

6 #76720

A Journey For Two, By Caribou!
Issued: 1998 • Current
Original Price: $22.50
Market Value: $22.50

7 #76449

Just One Little Candle
Issued: 1992 • Retired: 1998
Original Price: $7
Market Value: $15

8 #76554

Let's All Chime In!
(set/2)
Issued: 1993 • Retired: 1998
Original Price: $20
Market Value: $22

Pewter Miniatures		
	Price Paid	Value
1.		
2.		
3.		
4.		
5.		
6.		
7.		
8.		
Totals		

1 #76643

Let's Go Skating
Issued: 1994 • Retired: 1999
Original Price: $7
Market Value: $9

2 #76368

Let's Go Skiing
Issued: 1992 • Retired: 1999
Original Price: $7
Market Value: $9

3 #76678

**Lift Me Higher,
I Can't Reach! (set/5)**
Issued: 1994 • Retired: 1997
Original Price: $25
Market Value: $30

4 #76733

New!

Make A Wish
Issued: 1999 • Current
Original Price: $15
Market Value: $15

5 #76699

Mush! (set/2)
Issued: 1995 • Current
Original Price: $25
Market Value: $25

6 #76734

New!

**My Snowbaby
Baby Dolls (set/2)**
Issued: 1999 • Current
Original Price: $15
Market Value: $15

Pewter Miniatures

	Price Paid	Value
1.		
2.		
3.		
4.		
5.		
6.		
7.		
8.		
Totals		

7 #76728

New Frosty Frolic Land
(accessory)
Issued: 1998 • Current
Original Price: $50
Market Value: $50

8 #76570

**Now I Lay Me Down
To Sleep**
Issued: 1993 • Current
Original Price: $7
Market Value: $7

Value Guide — Department 56® Snowbabies™

1 #76724

**One For You,
One For Me**
Issued: 1998 • Current
Original Price: $13.50
Market Value: $13.50

2 #76163

Penguin Parade (set/4)
Issued: 1989 • Retired: 1993
Original Price: $12.50
Market Value: $31

3 #76236

Playing Games Is Fun!
(set/2)
Issued: 1990 • Retired: 1993
Original Price: $13.50
Market Value: $32

4 #76090

Polar Express (set/2)
Issued: 1989 • Retired: 1992
Original Price: $13.50
Market Value: $34

5 #76740

New!

Pull Together (set/3)
Issued: 1999 • Current
Original Price: $25
Market Value: $25

6 #76228

Read Me A Story!
Issued: 1990 • Retired: 1997
Original Price: $11
Market Value: $18

7 #76692

**Ring The Bells . . .
It's Christmas!**
Issued: 1995 • Current
Original Price: $20
Market Value: $20

8 #76422

Shall I Play For You?
Issued: 1992 • Retired: 1998
Original Price: $7
Market Value: $10

Pewter Miniatures

	Price Paid	Value
1.		
2.		
3.		
4.		
5.		
6.		
7.		
8.		

Totals

1 #76726

Ship O' Dreams (set/2)
Issued: 1998 • Current
Original Price: $45
Market Value: $45

2 #76737

New!

Slip, Sliding Away
Issued: 1999 • Current
Original Price: $12
Market Value: $12

3 #76686

**Snowbabies Animated
Skating Pond (set/14)**
Issued: 1995 • Retired: 1998
Original Price: $60
Market Value: $62

4 #76562

**Somewhere In
Dreamland (set/5)**
Issued: 1993 • Retired: 1997
Original Price: $30
Market Value: $40

5 #76244

A Special Delivery
Issued: 1990 • Retired: 1993
Original Price: $7
Market Value: $21

6 #76698

A Star-In-The-Box
Issued: 1995 • Retired: 1998
Original Price: $7.50
Market Value: $10

Pewter Miniatures

	Price Paid	Value
1.		
2.		
3.		
4.		
5.		
6.		
7.		
8.		

Totals

7 #76714

Starlight Serenade
Issued: 1997 • Current
Original Price: $12
Market Value: $12

8 #76651

Stringing Fallen Stars
Issued: 1994 • Retired: 1998
Original Price: $8
Market Value: $12

1   #76738

New!

Stuck In The Snow
Issued: 1999 • Current
Original Price: $16.50
Market Value: $16.50

2   #76715

Thank You (set/3)
Issued: 1997 • Current
Original Price: $20
Market Value: $20

3   #76619

There's Another One
Issued: 1994 • Retired: 1997
Original Price: $10
Market Value: $12

4   #76708

**There's No Place
Like Home**
Issued: 1996 • Retired: 1999
Original Price: $7.50
Market Value: $9

5   #76392

This Will Cheer You Up
Issued: 1992 • Retired: 1995
Original Price: $13.75
Market Value: $20

6   #76725

**Three Tiny Trumpeters
(set/2)**
Issued: 1998 • Current
Original Price: $25
Market Value: $25

7   #76155

Tiny Trio (set/3)
Issued: 1989 • Retired: 1993
Original Price: $18
Market Value: $32

8   #76736

New!

To My Friend
Issued: 1999 • Current
Original Price: $7.50
Market Value: $7.50

Pewter Miniatures

	Price Paid	Value
1.		
2.		
3.		
4.		
5.		
6.		
7.		
8.		

Totals

1   #76147

Tumbling In The Snow!
(set/5)
Issued: 1989 • Retired: 1992
Original Price: $30
Market Value: $72

2   #76210

Twinkle Little Stars
(set/2)
Issued: 1990 • Retired: 1993
Original Price: $15
Market Value: $32

3   #76414

Wait For Me! (set/4)
Issued: 1992 • Retired: 1995
Original Price: $22.50
Market Value: $30

4   #76295

Waiting For Christmas
Issued: 1991 • Retired: 1993
Original Price: $12.50
Market Value: $26

5   #76520

We Make A Great Pair
Issued: 1993 • Retired: 1997
Original Price: $13.50
Market Value: $17

6   #76635

We'll Plant The Starry Pines (set/4)
Issued: 1994 • Retired: 1997
Original Price: $22
Market Value: $25

Pewter Miniatures

	Price Paid	Value
1.		
2.		
3.		
4.		
5.		
6.		
7.		
8.		
Totals		

7   #76697

8   #76693

We're Building An Icy Igloo (set/3)
Issued: 1995 • Current
Original Price: $27.50
Market Value: $27.50

What Shall We Do Today? (set/2)
Issued: 1995 • Retired: 1999
Original Price: $17
Market Value: $17

Value Guide — Department 56® Snowbabies™

1   #76707

When The Bough Breaks
Issued: 1996 • Current
Original Price: $18
Market Value: $18

2   #76546

Where Did He Go?
(set/4)
Issued: 1993 • Current
Original Price: $20
Market Value: $20

3   #76701

Which Way's Up?
(set/2)
Issued: 1996 • Current
Original Price: $13.50
Market Value: $13.50

4   #76712

Whistle While You Work
Issued: 1997 • Current
Original Price: $18
Market Value: $18

5   #76252

Why Don't You Talk To Me? (set/2)
Issued: 1991 • Current
Original Price: $12
Market Value: $12

6   #76538

Will It Snow Today?
(set/5)
Issued: 1993 • Retired: 1998
Original Price: $22.50
Market Value: $25

7   #76589

Winken, Blinken & Nod
(set/2)
Issued: 1993 • Retired: 1998
Original Price: $27.50
Market Value: $30

8   #76727

Winter Play On A Snowy Day (set/4)
Issued: 1998 • Current
Original Price: $27.50
Market Value: $27.50

Pewter Miniatures

	Price Paid	Value
1.		
2.		
3.		
4.		
5.		
6.		
7.		
8.		
Totals		

1 #76074

Winter Surprise!
Issued: 1989 • Retired: 1994
Original Price: $13.50
Market Value: $26

2 #76717

**Wish Upon
A Falling Star (set/4)**
Issued: 1997 • Current
Original Price: $25
Market Value: $25

3 #76260

Wishing On A Star
Issued: 1991 • Retired: 1995
Original Price: $10
Market Value: $26

4 #76704

**With Hugs & Kisses
(set/2)**
Issued: 1996 • Retired: 1998
Original Price: $15
Market Value: $24

5 #76703

**You Are My Lucky Star
(set/2)**
Issued: 1996 • Current
Original Price: $20
Market Value: $20

6 #76732

New!

You Are My Starshine
Issued: 1999 • Current
Original Price: $7.50
Market Value: $7.50

Pewter Miniatures

	Price Paid	Value
1.		
2.		
3.		
4.		
5.		
6.		
7.		
8.		

Totals

7 #76376

**You Can't Find Me!
(set/4)**
Issued: 1992 • Retired: 1996
Original Price: $22.50
Market Value: $32

8 #76430

**You Didn't Forget Me!
(set/3)**
Issued: 1992 • Retired: 1995
Original Price: $17.50
Market Value: $25

1 #76709

You Need Wings Too!
(set/2)
Issued: 1996 • Current
Original Price: $11
Market Value: $11

Hinged Boxes

2 #68847

Celebrate
Issued: 1997 • Retired: 1999
Original Price: $15
Market Value: N/E

3 #68949

Fly With Me
Issued: 1999 • Current
Original Price: $15
Market Value: $15

4 #68948

Hard Landing
Issued: 1999 • Current
Original Price: $15
Market Value: $15

5 #68884

Hold On Tight
Issued: 1998 • Retired: 1999
Original Price: $15
Market Value: $15

6 #68867

I Love You
(Mother's Day
1997 event piece)
Issued: 1997 • Retired: 1998
Original Price: $15
Market Value: $17

7 #68928

I'll Ring For You
Issued: 1998 • Current
Original Price: $15
Market Value: $15

Pewter Miniatures	
Price Paid	Value
1.	

Hinged Boxes	
2.	
3.	
4.	
5.	
6.	
7.	
Totals	

1 #68929

Just Imagine
Issued: 1998 • Current
Original Price: $15
Market Value: $15

2 #68883

Once Upon A Time . . .
Issued: 1998 • Current
Original Price: $15
Market Value: $15

3 #68869

Polar Express
Issued: 1997 • Current
Original Price: $15
Market Value: $15

4 #69030

New!

Reach Out
Issued: 1999 • Current
Original Price: $17.50
Market Value: $17.50

5 #68848

Rock-A-Bye Baby
(10th Anniversary
1997 event piece)
Issued: 1997 • Retired: 1997
Original Price: $15
Market Value: $20

6 #69027

New!

Sending Hugs To You
(Spring Promotion
2000 event piece)
Issued: 1999 • Current
Original Price: $15
Market Value: $15

Hinged Boxes

	Price Paid	Value
1.		
2.		
3.		
4.		
5.		
6.		
7.		
8.		

Totals

7 #69029

New!

Super Star
Issued: 1999 • Current
Original Price: $15
Market Value: $15

8 #68846

Surprise
Issued: 1997 • Current
Original Price: $15
Market Value: $15

1 #68868

Sweet Dreams
Issued: 1997 • Current
Original Price: $15
Market Value: $15

2 #68930

Sweet Heart
(Mother's Day
1999 event piece)
Issued: 1998 • Retired: 1999
Original Price: $15
Market Value: $15

3 #69028

New!

Take The First Step
Issued: 1999 • Current
Original Price: $15
Market Value: $15

4 #68947

Time Out
Issued: 1999 • Current
Original Price: $15
Market Value: $15

Musicals & Waterglobes

5 #79375

All Tired Out
♪ *"Brahms' Lullaby"*
Issued: 1990 • Retired: 1992
Original Price: $55
Market Value: $72

6 #68797

Are You On My List?
♪ *"Have Yourself A
Merry Little Christmas"*
Issued: 1995 • Retired: 1997
Original Price: $32.50
Market Value: $37

7 #76481

Can I Open It Now?
♪ *"Happy Birthday"*
Issued: 1993 • Retired: 1994
Original Price: $20
Market Value: $38

Hinged Boxes		
	Price Paid	Value
1.		
2.		
3.		
4.		
Musicals & Waterglobes		
5.		
6.		
7.		
Totals		

Snowbabies™

1 #68713

Catch A Falling Star
♪ *"Catch A Falling Star"*
Issued: 1994 • Retired: 1997
Original Price: $37.50
Market Value: $42

2 #79677

Catch A Falling Star
♪ *"Catch A Falling Star"*
Issued: 1986 • Retired: 1987
Original Price: $18
Market Value: $645

3 #68870

Did He See You?
♪ *"Winter Wonderland"*
Issued: 1997 • Current
Original Price: $37.50
Market Value: $37.50

4 #79723

Don't Fall Off!
♪ *"When You Wish Upon A Star"*
Issued: 1987 • Retired: 1993
Original Price: $30
Market Value: $55

5 #68322

Fishing For Dreams
♪ *"Catch A Falling Star"*
Issued: 1992 • Retired: 1994
Original Price: $32.50
Market Value: $60

6 #76341

Frosty Frolic
♪ *"Let It Snow"*
Issued: 1991 • Retired: 1993
Original Price: $110
Market Value: $175

Musicals & Waterglobes

	Price Paid	Value
1.		
2.		
3.		
4.		
5.		
6.		
7.		
8.		
Totals		

7 #76503

Frosty Fun
♪ *"Frosty The Snowman"*
Issued: 1993 • Retired: 1994
Original Price: $20
Market Value: $38

8 #68872

Heigh-Ho
♪ *"Heigh-Ho"*
Issued: 1997 • Retired: 1999
Original Price: $32.50
Market Value: $34

Value Guide – Department 56® Snowbabies™

1 #68921

**I Love You From The
Bottom Of My Heart**
(Mother's Day
1999 event piece)
♪ *"What The World
Needs Now Is Love"*
Issued: 1998 • Retired: 1999
Original Price: $30
Market Value: $30

2 #68798

I'll Hug You Goodnight
♪ *"Frosty The Snowman"*
Issued: 1995 • Current
Original Price: $32.50
Market Value: $32.50

3 #68519

I'm So Sleepy
(revolving)
♪ *"Brahms' Lullaby"*
Issued: 1993 • Current
Original Price: $37.50
Market Value: $37.50

4 #68871

Jingle Bell
♪ *"Jingle Bells"*
Issued: 1997 • Retired: 1999
Original Price: $32.50
Market Value: $34

5 #68916

Just Follow The Star
♪ *"Twinkle, Twinkle,
Little Star"*
Issued: 1998 • Current
Original Price: $48
Market Value: $48

6 #68578

Let It Snow
(animated)
♪ *"Let It Snow"*
Issued: 1993 • Retired: 1995
Original Price: $100
Market Value: $120

7 #79928

Let It Snow
♪ *"Winter Wonderland"*
Issued: 1989 • Retired: 1993
Original Price: $25
Market Value: $48

8 #68721

Look What I Found!
♪ *"Winter Wonderland"*
Issued: 1994 • Retired: 1997
Original Price: $32.50
Market Value: $38

Musicals & Waterglobes

	Price Paid	Value
1.		
2.		
3.		
4.		
5.		
6.		
7.		
8.		
Totals		

1 #69040

New!

Make A Wish
♪ *"Happy Birthday To You"*
Issued: 1999 • Current
Original Price: $32.50
Market Value: $32.50

2 #68873

Moon Beams
♪ *"Rock-A-Bye Baby"*
Issued: 1997 • Retired: 1999
Original Price: $32.50
Market Value: $34

3 #68831

**Now I Lay Me
Down To Sleep**
♪ *"Brahms' Lullaby"*
Issued: 1996 • Current
Original Price: $32.50
Market Value: $32.50

4 #68832

Once Upon A Time . . .
(Mother's Day 1997 event
piece, moving figurine)
♪ *"When You Wish
Upon A Star"*
Issued: 1996 • Retired: 1999
Original Price: $30
Market Value: $36

5 #79383

Peek-A-Boo
♪ *"Jingle Bells"*
Issued: 1991 • Retired: 1993
Original Price: $50
Market Value: $80

6 #76333

Penguin Parade
♪ *"Brahms' Lullaby"*
Issued: 1991 • Retired: 1994
Original Price: $72
Market Value: $80

**Musicals &
Waterglobes**

	Price Paid	Value
1.		
2.		
3.		
4.		
5.		
6.		
7.		
8.		

Totals

7 #76465

Penguin Parade
♪ *"Winter Wonderland"*
Issued: 1993 • Retired: 1994
Original Price: $20
Market Value: $42

8 #68705

Planting Starry Pines
♪ *"O Tannenbaum"*
Issued: 1994 • Retired: 1996
Original Price: $32.50
Market Value: $42

1 #68809

Play Me A Tune
♪ *"Little Drummer Boy"*
Issued: 1995 • Retired: 1998
Original Price: $37.50
Market Value: $72

2 #76511

Play Me A Tune
♪ *"Joy To The World"*
Issued: 1993 • Retired: 1994
Original Price: $20
Market Value: $40

3 #79367

Play Me A Tune
♪ *"We Wish You
A Merry Christmas"*
Issued: 1991 • Retired: 1993
Original Price: $50
Market Value: $70

4 #76325

Playing Games Is Fun!
(revolving)
♪ *"Twinkle, Twinkle,
Little Star"*
Issued: 1991 • Retired: 1993
Original Price: $72
Market Value: $109

5 #68830

Practice Makes Perfect
♪ *"Twinkle, Twinkle,
Little Star"*
Issued: 1996 • Retired: 1998
Original Price: $32.50
Market Value: $34

6 #68314

Read Me A Story!
♪ *"Twinkle, Twinkle,
Little Star"*
Issued: 1992 • Retired: 1996
Original Price: $32.50
Market Value: $40

7 #76490

Reading A Story
♪ *"Brahms' Lullaby"*
Issued: 1993 • Retired: 1994
Original Price: $20
Market Value: $42

8 #68915

Ship Ahoy
♪ *"Row, Row, Row"*
Issued: 1998 • Current
Original Price: $37.50
Market Value: $37.50

Musicals & Waterglobes

	Price Paid	Value
1.		
2.		
3.		
4.		
5.		
6.		
7.		
8.		

Totals

81

1 #69039

New!

Ship O' Dreams
Issued: 1999 • Current
Original Price: $75
Market Value: $75

2 #68799

Skate With Me
♪ "Skaters Waltz"
Issued: 1995 • Retired: 1998
Original Price: $32.50
Market Value: $35

3 #68833

**Sliding Through
The Milky Way**
♪ "Twinkle, Twinkle,
Little Star"
Issued: 1996 • Retired: 1999
Original Price: $37.50
Market Value: $39

4 #76350

**Snowbabies Advent
Tree w/24 Ornaments**
♪ "We Wish You
A Merry Christmas"
Issued: 1991 • Retired: 1994
Original Price: $135
Market Value: $192

5 #79758

**Snowbabies
Riding Sleds**
♪ "Winter Wonderland"
Issued: 1987 • Retired: 1988
Original Price: $40
Market Value: $750

6 #79502

**Snowbaby Porcelain
Music Box**
♪ "Catch A Falling Star"
Issued: 1986 • Retired: 1987
Original Price: $27.50
Market Value: $625

Musicals & Waterglobes

	Price Paid	Value
1.		
2.		
3.		
4.		
5.		
6.		
7.		
8.		

Totals

7 #79642

Snowbaby Standing
Issued: 1986 • Retired: 1987
Original Price: $7.50
Market Value: $455

8 #79731

Snowbaby With Wings
(lighted)
Issued: 1987 • Retired: 1988
Original Price: $20
Market Value: $430

1 #68497

So Much Work To Do!
♪ *"Whistle While You Work"*
Issued: 1993 • Retired: 1995
Original Price: $32.50
Market Value: $42

2 #68953

Swing Your Partner
(Parkwest early release)
♪ *"Shall We Dance?"*
Issued: 1999 • Current
Original Price: $37.50
Market Value: $37.50

3 #69041

New!

That's What Friends Are For (animated)
♪ *"That's What Friends Are For"*
Issued: 1999 • Current
Original Price: $45
Market Value: $45

4 #79359

What Are You Doing?
(never released due to production problems)
♪ *"Twinkle, Twinkle, Little Star"*
Issued: 1990 • Retired: 1990
Original Price: $55
Market Value: N/A

5 #68268

What Will I Catch?
♪ *"Catch A Falling Star"*
Issued: 1992 • Retired: 1998
Original Price: $48
Market Value: $50

6 #76473

Wishing On A Star
♪ *"When You Wish Upon A Star"*
Issued: 1993 • Retired: 1994
Original Price: $20
Market Value: $40

7 #68500

You Didn't Forget Me!
♪ *"Have Yourself A Merry Little Christmas"*
Issued: 1993 • Retired: 1997
Original Price: $32.50
Market Value: $38

8 #68955

You're My Best Partner
(Parade of Gifts early release)
♪ *"I Could Have Danced All Night"*
Issued: 1999 • Current
Original Price: $32.50
Market Value: $32.50

Musicals & Waterglobes

	Price Paid	Value
1.		
2.		
3.		
4.		
5.		
6.		
7.		
8.		
Totals		

Other Snowbabies Collectibles

1 #77305

Allison & Duncan
(set/2, papier-maché dolls)
Issued: 1988 • Retired: 1989
Original Price: $200
Market Value: $870

2 #68462

Baby's First Smile
Issued: 1993 • Retired: 1998
Original Price: $30
Market Value: $30

3 #68863

Candle Light . . . Season Bright (tree topper)
Issued: 1997 • Retired: 1999
Original Price: $20
Market Value: $20

4 #69025

New!

Candle Lights (set/6)
Issued: 1999 • Current
Original Price: $15
Market Value: $15

5 #68861

Candlelight Trees (set/3)
Issued: 1997 • Retired: 1999
Original Price: $25
Market Value: $25

Other Snowbabies Collectibles

	Price Paid	Value
1.		
2.		
3.		
4.		
5.		
6.		
Totals		

6 #68837

Display Your Favorite Snowbaby Lamp
Issued: 1996 • Retired: 1998
Original Price: $45
Market Value: $45

Value Guide — Department 56® Snowbabies™

1   #79634

Frosty Forest (set/2)
Issued: 1986 • Current
Original Price: $15
Market Value: $20

2   #76687

Frosty Pines (set/3)
Issued: 1995 • Retired: 1998
Original Price: $12.50
Market Value: $12.50

3   #68862

**I'm The Star Atop
Your Tree! (tree topper)**
Issued: 1997 • Retired: 1999
Original Price: $20
Market Value: $20

4   #69024

New!

Icebergs (set/3)
Issued: 1999 • Current
Original Price: $20
Market Value: $20

5   #79871

Icy Igloo (lighted)
Is sued: 1989 • Current
Original Price: $37.50
Market Value: $37.50

6   #68836

A Little Night Light
Issued: 1996 • Retired: 1999
Original Price: $75
Market Value: $75

7   #68938

Mirrored Display Unit
Issued: 1998 • Current
Original Price: $65
Market Value: $65

8   #69023

New!

Moon Ornament Hanger
Issued: 1999 • Current
Original Price: $6.50
Market Value: $6.50

Other Snowbabies Collectibles

	Price Paid	Value
1.		
2.		
3.		
4.		
5.		
6.		
7.		
8.		

Totals

1 #68835

Moonbeams (night light)
Issued: 1996 • Retired: 1999
Original Price: $20
Market Value: $20

2 #68815

Once Upon A Time . . .
(votive cup & candle)
Issued: 1996 • Current
Original Price: $25
Market Value: $25

3 #68284

Over The Milky Way
Issued: 1992 • Retired: 1995
Original Price: $32
Market Value: $42

4 #68640

Pennies From Heaven
(bank)
Issued: 1994 • Retired: 1998
Original Price: $17.50
Market Value: $17.50

5 #68849

**Snowbabies 1997
Bisque Friendship Pin**
(10th Anniversary
event piece)
Issued: 1997 • Retired: 1997
Original Price: $5
Market Value: $8

6 #N/A

Snowbabies Bookmark
(free gift with purchase of
Mother's Day 1999
musical event piece)
Issued: N/A • Retired: N/A
Original Price: N/A
Market Value: N/E

Other Snowbabies Collectibles

	Price Paid	Value
1.		
2.		
3.		
4.		
5.		
6.		
7.		
Totals		

7 #79669

**Snowbabies
Hanging Pair**
(set/2, glass votive and
candle not included)
Issued: 1986 • Retired: 1989
Original Price: $15
Market Value: $170

86

1   #69026

New!

**Snowbabies
Landscape Set (set/7)**
Issued: 1999 • Current
Original Price: $15
Market Value: $15

2   #68047

Snowbabies Polar Sign
Issued: 1991 • Retired: 1996
Original Price: $20
Market Value: $28

3   #79650

**Snowbaby
Climbing On Snowball
(bisque votive w/candle)**
Issued: 1986 • Retired: 1989
Original Price: $15
Market Value: $122

4   #68838

Snowbaby Display Sled
Issued: 1996 • Current
Original Price: $45
Market Value: $45

5   #79707

**Snowbaby Holding
Picture Frame (set/2)**
Issued: 1986 • Retired: 1987
Original Price: $15
Market Value: $575

6   #79596

Snowbaby Nite Lite
Issued: 1986 • Retired: 1989
Original Price: $15
Market Value: $365

7   #68874

Snowbaby Shelf Unit
Issued: 1997 • Retired: 1999
Original Price: $20
Market Value: $20

8   #69046

New!

Snowy Pines (set/3)
Issued: 1999 • Current
Original Price: $8.50
Market Value: $8.50

Other Snowbabies Collectibles

	Price Paid	Value
1.		
2.		
3.		
4.		
5.		
6.		
7.		
8.		

Totals

Snowbabies™

1 #68936

Star Base Display Tree
(miniature)
Issued: 1998 • Current
Original Price: $30
Market Value: $30

2 #85336

New!

**Star Base
Ornament Hanger**
Issued: 1999 • Current
Original Price: $7.50
Market Value: $7.50

3 #68952

Star On The Top
(tree topper)
Issued: 1999 • Current
Original Price: $12.50
Market Value: $12.50

4 #68292

Starry Pines (set/2)
Issued: 1992 • Retired: 1998
Original Price: $17.50
Market Value: $20

5 #69022

New!

Tower Of Light
Issued: 1999 • Current
Original Price: $40
Market Value: $40

6 #68887

**Winter Celebration
Event Pin**
(Winter Celebration
1998 event piece)
Issued: 1998 • Retired: 1998
Original Price: $5
Market Value: $7

**Other Snowbabies
Collectibles**

	Price Paid	Value
1.		
2.		
3.		
4.		
5.		
6.		
7.		

Totals

7 #68834

You're My Snowbaby
Issued: 1996 • Retired: 1999
Original Price: $15
Market Value: $15

Snowbabies Friendship Club

The creation of the Snowbabies Friendship Club in 1997 has given collectors an exciting new way to show their love for Snowbabies. If you're not a member yet, there's no time like the present to join.

1 #730002
#682005

1998

Friendship Pin/Charter Charm And Star Charm
Issued: 1997 • Current
Original Price: N/A
Market Value: N/E

2 #720003

1998

Illustration With Frame
Issued: 1997 • Current
Original Price: N/A
Market Value: N/E

3 #68852

1998

Together We Can Make The Season Bright
Issued: 1997 • Retired: 1998
Original Price: $75
Market Value: $75

4 #710004

1998

You Better Watch Out!
Issued: 1997 • Current
Original Price: N/A
Market Value: N/E

5 #68889

1999

Baby, It's Cold Outside
(set/2)
Issued: 1998 • Retired: 1999
Original Price: N/A
Market Value: N/E

6 #68889

1999

Friendship Pin/Charms
(penguin charm for renewing members, star charm for new members)
Issued: 1998 • Retired: 1999
Original Price: N/A
Market Value: N/E

Club Pieces

	Price Paid	Value
1.		
2.		
3.		
4.		
5.		
6.		

Totals

Snowbabies Friendship Club™

1   #68889

1999

Illustration With Frame
Issued: 1998 • Retired: 1999
Original Price: N/A
Market Value: N/E

2   #68898

1999

**Nice To Meet You
Little One (set/2)**
Issued: 1998 • Retired: 1999
Original Price: $75
Market Value: N/E

3   #6803

1999

You Better Watch Out
(renewal gift, hinged box)
To Be Issued: 1998 • Current
Original Price: N/A
Market Value: N/E

4   #68939A

New!

Celebrate Jinglebaby
(ornament)
Issued: 1999 • Current
Original Price: N/A
Market Value: N/E

5   #N/A

New!

Friendship Charms
(set/5, renewal gift)
Issued: 1999 • Current
Original Price: N/A
Market Value: N/E

6   #68939B

New!

Sailing The Seas
Issued: 1999 • Current
Original Price: N/A
Market Value: N/E

Club Pieces

	Price Paid	Value
1.		
2.		
3.		
4.		
5.		
6.		
7.		
8.		

Totals

7   #68939C

New!

Star Bright (pin)
Issued: 1999 • Current
Original Price: N/A
Market Value: N/E

8   #68956

New!

Storytime
(comes with story booklet)
Issued: 1999 • Current
Original Price: $50
Market Value: $50

#26341

**Afternoon
In The Garden**
(resin bench w/tree)
Issued: 1999 • Current
Original Price: $32.50
Market Value: $32.50

Snowbunnies

Since hopping its way into the hearts of collectors in 1994, the Snowbunnies line has continued to grow in number and popularity. In addition to figurines, there are also water-globes, music boxes and hinged boxes to add to your springtime collection.

#26288

**All The Little Birdies Go,
"Tweet, Tweet, Tweet!"**
(set/2)
Issued: 1997 • Current
Original Price: $28
Market Value: $28

#26326

Animals On Parade
(set/4)
Issued: 1999 • Current
Original Price: $17.50
Market Value: $17.50

#26308

**April Brings
May Flowers**
Issued: 1998 • Current
Original Price: $35
Market Value: $35

#26289

Are You My Momma?
Issued: 1997 • Current
Original Price: $18
Market Value: $18

#26287

Bunny Express
Issued: 1997 • Current
Original Price: $22.50
Market Value: $22.50

Figurines	Price Paid	Value
1.		
2.		
3.		
4.		
5.		
6.		
Totals		

1 #26327

Bunny Hug
Issued: 1999 • Current
Original Price: $25
Market Value: $25

2 #26322

Butterfly Kisses
Issued: 1999 • Current
Original Price: $20
Market Value: $20

3 #26309

**Can You Come Out
& Play?** (LE-1999)
Issued: 1998 • Retired: 1999
Original Price: $25
Market Value: $32

4 #26282

**Counting The Days
'Til Easter** (LE-1997)
Issued: 1996 • Retired: 1997
Original Price: $22.50
Market Value: $40

5 #26166

Don't Get Lost!
Issued: 1995 • Retired: 1998
Original Price: $32.50
Market Value: $36

6 #26293

Double Yolk (LE-1998)
Issued: 1997 • Retired: 1998
Original Price: $20
Market Value: $30

Figurines	
Price Paid	Value
1.	
2.	
3.	
4.	
5.	
6.	
7.	
8.	
Totals	

7 #26085

Easter Delivery
Issued: 1994 • Retired: 1997
Original Price: $27.50
Market Value: $30

8 #26274

Easy Does It (set/2)
Issued: 1996 • Retired: 1998
Original Price: $30
Market Value: $33

1 #26324

Ewe Haul
Issued: 1999 • Current
Original Price: $20
Market Value: $20

2 #26329

Full Of Blooms (set/6)
Issued: 1999 • Current
Original Price: $15
Market Value: $15

3 #26328

Garden Park Bench
Issued: 1999 • Current
Original Price: $15
Market Value: $15

4 #26340

Garden Picket Fence
(set/4)
Issued: 1999 • Current
Original Price: $30
Market Value: $30

5 #26174

Goosey, Goosey & Gander (set/2)
Issued: 1995 • Retired: 1997
Original Price: $30
Market Value: $42

6 #26325

Guests Are Always Welcome (LE-2000)
Issued: 1999 • Current
Original Price: $25
Market Value: $25

7 #26273

Happy Birthday To You
(set/2)
Issued: 1996 • Current
Original Price: $30
Market Value: $30

8 #26077

Help Me Hide The Eggs
Issued: 1994 • Retired: 1996
Original Price: $25
Market Value: $38

Figurines		
	Price Paid	Value
1.		
2.		
3.		
4.		
5.		
6.		
7.		
8.		
	Totals	

1 #26301

Hop Skip & A Melody
(set/2)
Issued: 1998 • Current
Original Price: $30
Market Value: $30

2 #26302

I Can Do It Myself
Issued: 1998 • Current
Original Price: $16.50
Market Value: $16.50

3 #26212

I'll Color The Easter Egg
(LE-1996)
Issued: 1995 • Retired: 1996
Original Price: $20
Market Value: $35

4 #26158

I'll Love You Forever
Issued: 1995 • Current
Original Price: $16
Market Value: $16

5 #26034

I'll Paint The Top . . .
Issued: 1994 • Retired: 1996
Original Price: $30
Market Value: $40

6 #26204

I'm Teeter, You're Totter
Issued: 1995 • Retired: 1998
Original Price: $30
Market Value: $33

Figurines

	Price Paid	Value
1.		
2.		
3.		
4.		
5.		
6.		
7.		
8.		

Totals

7 #26272

I've Got A Brand New Pair Of Roller Skates
Issued: 1996 • Retired: 1998
Original Price: $25
Market Value: $25

8 #26000

I've Got A Surprise!
Issued: 1994 • Retired: 1997
Original Price: $15
Market Value: $25

1 #26275

Is There Room For Me?
Issued: 1996 • Retired: 1999
Original Price: $18
Market Value: $20

2 #26190

It's Working . . . We're Going Faster!
Issued: 1995 • Retired: 1999
Original Price: $35
Market Value: $38

3 #26278

Just A Little Off The Top (set/3)
Issued: 1996 • Retired: 1998
Original Price: $25
Market Value: $28

4 #26323

Just For You
Issued: 1999 • Current
Original Price: $16.50
Market Value: $16.50

5 #26304

Just Start All Over Again
Issued: 1998 • Current
Original Price: $16.50
Market Value: $16.50

6 #26276

Let's All Sing Like The Birdies Sing (set/2)
Issued: 1996 • Retired: 1999
Original Price: $37.50
Market Value: $37.50

7 #26093

Let's Do The Bunny-Hop!
Issued: 1994 • Current
Original Price: $32.50
Market Value: $32.50

8 #26303

Loves Me, Loves Me Not
Issued: 1998 • Current
Original Price: $16.50
Market Value: $16.50

Figurines		
	Price Paid	Value
1.		
2.		
3.		
4.		
5.		
6.		
7.		
8.		
Totals		

Snowbunnies®

1   #26321

Master Gardner (set/4)
Issued: 1999 • Current
Original Price: $20
Market Value: $20

2   #26255

**My Woodland Wagon,
At Dragonfly Hollow**
(lighted)
Issued: 1995 • Retired: 1997
Original Price: $32.50
Market Value: $33

3   #26239

**My Woodland Wagon,
By Turtle Creek (lighted)**
Issued: 1995 • Retired: 1996
Original Price: $32.50
Market Value: $45

4   #26247

**My Woodland Wagon,
Parked In Robins Nest
Thicket (set/2, lighted)**
Issued: 1995 • Retired: 1999
Original Price: $35
Market Value: $38

5   #26283

**On A Tricycle Built For
Two (LE-17,500)**
Issued: 1996 • Retired: 1998
Original Price: $32.50
Market Value: $59

6   #26018

Oops! I Dropped One!
Issued: 1994 • Retired: 1998
Original Price: $16
Market Value: $22

7   #26291

Rain, Rain, Go Away!
Issued: 1997 • Current
Original Price: $45
Market Value: $45

Figurines	Price Paid	Value
1.		
2.		
3.		
4.		
5.		
6.		
7.		
Totals		

1 #26306

Rock-A-Bye Bunny
Issued: 1998 • Current
Original Price: $22.50
Market Value: $22.50

2 #26115

Rub-A-Dub-Dub, Three Bunnies In A Tub
Issued: 1995 • Retired: 1997
Original Price: $32
Market Value: $43

3 #26131

Shrubs-In-A-Tub
Issued: 1995 • Retired: 1997
Original Price: $10
Market Value: $10

4 #26140

Shrubs-In-A-Tub (set/2)
Issued: 1995 • Retired: 1997
Original Price: $9
Market Value: $15

5 #26123

Shrubs-In-A-Tub (set/4)
Issued: 1995 • Retired: 1997
Original Price: $12.50
Market Value: $14

6 #26280

Slow-Moving Vehicle
Issued: 1996 • Retired: 1999
Original Price: $45
Market Value: $49

7 #26320

Stop & Smell The Roses (set/2)
Issued: 1999 • Current
Original Price: $20
Market Value: $20

8 #26042

Surprise! It's Me!
Issued: 1994 • Retired: 1998
Original Price: $25
Market Value: $30

	Figurines	
	Price Paid	Value
1.		
2.		
3.		
4.		
5.		
6.		
7.		
8.		
Totals		

Snowbunnies®

1 #26307

This One's A Keeper
Issued: 1998 • Current
Original Price: $16.50
Market Value: $16.50

2 #26026

A Tisket, A Tasket
Issued: 1994 • Retired: 1996
Original Price: $15
Market Value: $20

3 #26286

A Tisket Tasket Basket
Issued: 1997 • Current
Original Price: $45
Market Value: $45

4 #26281

To Market, To Market, Delivering Eggs! (set/3)
Issued: 1996 • Retired: 1999
Original Price: $65
Market Value: $68

5 #26069

Tra-La-La
Issued: 1994 • Retired: 1997
Original Price: $37.50
Market Value: $48

6 #26330

Trellis In Bloom
Issued: 1999 • Current
Original Price: $12.50
Market Value: $12.50

7 #26277

Welcome To The Neighborhood
Issued: 1996 • Retired: 1999
Original Price: $25
Market Value: $29

Figurines

	Price Paid	Value
1.		
2.		
3.		
4.		
5.		
6.		
7.		
Totals		

1 #26182

**Wishing You
A Happy Easter**
Issued: 1995 • Retired: 1997
Original Price: $32.50
Market Value: $40

2 #26220

**You Better Watch Out
Or I'll Catch You!**
Issued: 1995 • Retired: 1999
Original Price: $17
Market Value: $25

3 #26292

**You're Cute As
A Bug's Ear**
Issued: 1997 • Current
Original Price: $16.50
Market Value: $16.50

Hinged Boxes

4 #26298

Abracadabra
Issued: 1997 • Retired: 1999
Original Price: $15
Market Value: $16

5 #26313

Alleluia
Issued: 1998 • Current
Original Price: $20
Market Value: $20

6 #26332

Bunny In Bloom
Issued: 1999 • Current
Original Price: $15
Market Value: $15

7 #26331

Eye To Eye
Issued: 1999 • Current
Original Price: $15
Market Value: $15

Figurines	Price Paid	Value
1.		
2.		
3.		
Hinged Boxes		
4.		
5.		
6.		
7.		
Totals		

99

Snowbunnies®

1 — #26310

Happy Easter
Issued: 1998 • Current
Original Price: $15
Market Value: $15

2 — #26305

I Love You
Issued: 1998 • Current
Original Price: $15
Market Value: $15

3 — #26299

Piggyback?
Issued: 1997 • Current
Original Price: $15
Market Value: $15

4 — #26334

Sunny Side Up
Issued: 1999 • Current
Original Price: $15
Market Value: $15

5 — #26311

Sweet Dreams
Issued: 1998 • Current
Original Price: $15
Market Value: $15

6 — #26333

Sweet Violet
Issued: 1999 • Current
Original Price: $15
Market Value: $15

Hinged Boxes

	Price Paid	Value
1.		
2.		
3.		
4.		
5.		
6.		
7.		
8.		

Totals

7 — #26314

True Blue Friends
Issued: 1998 • Current
Original Price: $20
Market Value: $20

8 — #26297

Tweet, Tweet, Tweet
Issued: 1997 • Current
Original Price: $15
Market Value: $15

1 #26312

Two Of A Kind
Issued: 1998 • Current
Original Price: $20
Market Value: $20

Musicals
&
Waterglobes

2 #26290

And "B" Is For
Bunny (moving)
♪ *"Here Comes Peter*
Cottontail"
Issued: 1997 • Retired: 1999
Original Price: $30
Market Value: $30

3 #26294

Be My Baby
Bunny Bee (revolving)
♪ *"Honey"*
Issued: 1997 • Retired: 1999
Original Price: $32.50
Market Value: $34

4 #26295

Is There Room For Me?
♪ *"When The Red,*
Red Robin Comes . . ."
Issued: 1997 • Current
Original Price: $25
Market Value: $25

5 #26271

Let's Play
In The Meadow
♪ *"Oh! What A*
Beautiful Morning"
Issued: 1995 • Retired: 1998
Original Price: $25
Market Value: $25

6 #26337

Look For The Rainbow
♪ *"Raindrops Keep Falling*
On My Head"
Issued: 1999 • Current
Original Price: $32.50
Market Value: $32.50

7 #26263

Look What I've Got!
♪ *"Playmates"*
Issued: 1995 • Retired: 1997
Original Price: $25
Market Value: $25

Hinged Boxes		
	Price Paid	Value
1.		

Musicals & Waterglobes		
2.		
3.		
4.		
5.		
6.		
7.		

Totals

1  #26285

Rock-A-Bye Bunny
♪ *"Yes Sir That's My Baby"*
Issued: 1996 • Retired: 1999
Original Price: $25
Market Value: $25

2  #26338

Talk To The Animals
♪ *"Talk To The Animals"*
Issued: 1999 • Current
Original Price: $25
Market Value: $25

3  #26107

A Tisket, A Tasket
Issued: 1994 • Retired: 1998
Original Price: $12.50
Market Value: $14

4  #26284

You Make Me Laugh!
♪ *"Humoresque"*
Issued: 1996 • Retired: 1999
Original Price: $32.50
Market Value: $32.50

Musicals & Waterglobes	
Price Paid	Value
1.	
2.	
3.	
4.	
Totals	

Easter Collectibles

This annual series has bloomed every spring since 1990. Each of these bisque Easter critters is available in two sizes. The new 2000 figurines are a pair of delightful ducks who hope you'll welcome them into your home.

1 #73938

1990

Bisque Lamb (2.5")
Issued: 1990 • Retired: 1991
Original Price: $5
Market Value: $35

2 #73920

1990

Bisque Lamb (4")
Issued: 1990 • Retired: 1991
Original Price: $7.50
Market Value: $48

3 #74993

1991

Bisque Rabbit (4")
Issued: 1991 • Retired: 1992
Original Price: $6
Market Value: $20

4 #74985

1991

Bisque Rabbit (5")
Issued: 1991 • Retired: 1992
Original Price: $8
Market Value: $25

5 #72818

1992

Bisque Duckling (2.75")
Issued: 1992 • Retired: 1993
Original Price: $6.50
Market Value: $15

6 #72826

1992

Bisque Duckling (3.5")
Issued: 1992 • Retired: 1993
Original Price: $8.50
Market Value: $23

Figurines	
Price Paid	Value
1.	
2.	
3.	
4.	
5.	
6.	
Totals	

1   #24015

1993

Bisque Fledgling In A Nest (2.5")
Issued: 1993 • Retired: 1994
Original Price: $5
Market Value: $13

2   #24007

1993

Bisque Fledgling In A Nest (2.75")
Issued: 1993 • Retired: 1994
Original Price: $6
Market Value: $15

3   #24651

1994

Bisque Chick (2.75")
Issued: 1994 • Retired: 1995
Original Price: $6.50
Market Value: $15

4   #24643

1994

Bisque Chick (3.25")
Issued: 1994 • Retired: 1995
Original Price: $8.50
Market Value: $24

5   #27642

1995

Bisque Rabbit (3.75")
Issued: 1995 • Retired: 1996
Original Price: $7.50
Market Value: $7.50

6   #27650

1995

Bisque Rabbit (4.5")
Issued: 1995 • Retired: 1996
Original Price: $8.50
Market Value: $8.50

Figurines

	Price Paid	Value
1.		
2.		
3.		
4.		
5.		
6.		
7.		
8.		

Totals

7   #23701

1996

Bisque Rabbit (2.75")
Issued: 1996 • Retired: 1997
Original Price: $7.50
Market Value: $7.50

8   #23700

1996

Bisque Rabbit (3.5")
Issued: 1996 • Retired: 1997
Original Price: $8.50
Market Value: $8.50

Value Guide — Department 56® Easter Collectibles

1   #23774

1997

Bisque Pig (2.5")
Issued: 1997 • Retired: 1998
Original Price: $6.50
Market Value: $6.50

2   #23773

1997

Bisque Pig (3")
Issued: 1997 • Retired: 1998
Original Price: $7.50
Market Value: $15

3   #23861

1998

Bisque Kitten (2.5")
Issued: 1998 • Retired: 1999
Original Price: $6
Market Value: $6

4   #23862

1998

Bisque Kitten (3.5")
Issued: 1998 • Retired: 1999
Original Price: $7
Market Value: $7

5   #23902

1999

Bisque Duck (4.25")
Issued: 1999 • Current
Original Price: $7.50
Market Value: $7.50

6   #23901

1999

Bisque Duck (4.5")
Issued: 1999 • Current
Original Price: $8.50
Market Value: $8.50

Figurines

	Price Paid	Value
1.		
2.		
3.		
4.		
5.		
6.		
Totals		

Future Releases

Use this page to record future releases and purchases.

Snowbabies™	Item #	Status	Price Paid	Market Value

Snowbunnies®	Item #	Status	Price Paid	Market Value

Easter Collectibles	Item #	Status	Price Paid	Market Value

Page Total:	Price Paid	Value

Total Value Of My Collection

Record the Page Totals from the value guide section here.

Snowbabies™		
Page Number	Price Paid	Market Value
Page 29		
Page 30		
Page 31		
Page 32		
Page 33		
Page 34		
Page 35		
Page 36		
Page 37		
Page 38		
Page 39		
Page 40		
Page 41		
Page 42		
Page 43		
Page 44		
Page 45		
Page 46		
Page 47		
Page 48		
Page 49		
Page 50		
Page 51		
Page 52		
Page 53		
Page 54		
Page 55		
Page 56		
Page 57		
Page 58		
Page 59		
Page 60		
Page 61		
Page 62		
Page 63		
Page 64		
Page 65		
Page 66		
Page 67		
Page 68		
Subtotal		

Snowbabies™		
Page Number	Price Paid	Market Value
Page 69		
Page 70		
Page 71		
Page 72		
Page 73		
Page 74		
Page 75		
Page 76		
Page 77		
Page 78		
Page 79		
Page 80		
Page 81		
Page 82		
Page 83		
Page 84		
Page 85		
Page 86		
Page 87		
Page 88		
Page 89		
Page 90		

Snowbunnies®		
Page 91		
Page 92		
Page 93		
Page 94		
Page 95		
Page 96		
Page 97		
Page 98		
Page 99		
Page 100		
Page 101		
Page 102		

Easter Collectibles		
Page 103		
Page 104		
Page 105		
Subtotal		

Grand Total:	Price Paid	Value

❄ Secondary Market Overview ❄

As the Snowbabies collection heads into the new millennium, old pieces continue to retire, while eager new babies and bunnies enter the lineup. If a piece you desire happens to retire, don't fret! By examining your secondary market options, you may be able to track down that elusive piece for a price more reasonable than you might expect.

The Secondary Market Explained

What is the secondary market? It is where collectors turn when they seek a particular retired, limited edition or event piece that is no longer available from a retailer. Retired pieces are no longer produced by the manufacturer and the original molds are destroyed. Many pieces that have limited production runs or are only offered at particular events often see dramatic rises in values because there are not enough pieces for all the collectors who desire them. "Can I Help, Too?" was released in 1992 with an original price of $48. Today, the piece is worth nearly twice that amount. To see if you have a limited edition piece, turn your Snowbaby piece over. If it is numbered on the bottom, then it had a limited production run.

Finding a dealer or collector who has the particular piece you desire is not as difficult as it might seem. You may not have to look any further than your local newspaper. The classified section may list collectibles for sale, although you have a better chance of finding what you want through a source geared exclusively toward collectors. Sources such as secondary market exchanges and the Internet can put you in touch with an almost unlimited number of collectors all over the country, perhaps the world!

A secondary market exchange is a service that puts collectors who have pieces to sell in contact with those who wish to buy. With the exchange acting as a broker and receiving a fee from any sale, this method has long been the standard way of doing business on the secondary market. Typically, an exchange publishes a list or newsletter naming the pieces for sale. An advantage of going through an exchange is that the service takes away much of the legwork that is sometimes required when pursuing a particular piece.

For some collectors, the legwork is just as exciting and rewarding as acquiring the Snowbaby they desire. Collector functions such as swap meets are good places to check for retired Snowbabies. Here, you can meet both dealers and collectors, and they may be willing to negotiate lower prices in order to sell their wares. Even if you don't find your desired piece, the collectors you meet may know of other collectors who have it for sale.

The Popularity Of The Internet

In many respects, the Internet has taken away the need of dealing with a middleman. Collectors can now interact with other collectors at no charge by visiting web sites and chat rooms geared exclusively toward Snowbabies pieces. Long-lasting friendships can even develop between collectors who may live on opposite ends of the globe. And some of these new friends may even be willing to trade or sell the piece you need! The power of the Internet is liberating, but common sense must still be followed when dealing with strangers.

Simply typing the word "Snowbabies" into your Internet search engine should provide you with a number of web sites to begin your search. Some of these sites may be dealer or retailer sites, while others may have been created by and for Snowbabies fans just like yourself! One of the most popular places to start a search for a particular piece is at one of the many auction sites on the Internet.

Internet auction sites serve a similar role to secondary market exchanges. Here, buyers may bid on a particular piece they wish to acquire. The auction site often receives a percentage of the final selling price from the seller. When dealing through an auction, examine any photos that may be available of the object up for bid. Don't hesitate to voice your feelings, both positive and negative, if the auction site provides a system of ratings or feedback where both buyers and sellers can record their comments and complaints. It's a good idea to read over any feedback that might exist concerning the person you are preparing to buy from.

Snowbabies pieces are not only delightful collectibles, they are also fragile. When buying pieces over the Internet, ask if the piece you are planning to buy has been repaired. There is nothing wrong with buying a restored piece, but the secondary market price you pay should reflect the restored condition of the piece and, therefore, be lower. Other flaws that will decrease secondary market value are chips, blemishes and missing "nubbies" that cover the Snowbabies' suits.

Expect to see lower values for pieces that do not include their original boxes or other packaging. While pieces without boxes may have lower secondary market values, you may have the opportunity to purchase pieces at lower prices. Only you can determine if the piece being offered is worth the price being asked.

When To Buy Your Snowbabies

The winter-themed Snowbabies and spring-themed Snowbunnies may see their prices fluctuate during particular times of the year. And as the Christmas season approaches, prices may rise for particular Snowbabies. The same is true for Snowbunnies at Easter time. However, your chances of obtaining a particular piece may also be greater because more people may choose these times to sell their pieces.

The thrill of hunting down retired Snowbabies can be so exciting that it is easy to get caught up in speculation. Remember, values do not always go up. If you budget your money wisely and only buy pieces you enjoy, you will never be disappointed with your purchases.

Exchanges & Newsletters

Fifty-Six™
(formerly the *Quarterly*)
Department 56, Inc.
P.O. Box 44056
One Village Place
Eden Prairie, MN 55344-1056
(800) 548-8696
www.department56.com

56 Directions
Jeff & Susan McDermott
364 Spring Street Ext.
Glastonbury, CT 06033
(860) 633-8192
www.56directions.com

Collectible Exchange, Inc.
6621 Columbiana Road
New Middletown, OH 44442
(800) 752-3208
www.colexch.com

The Cottage Locator
Frank & Florence Wilson
211 No. Bridebrook Rd.
East Lyme, CT 06333
(860) 739-0705

Dickens' Exchange
Lynda W. Blankenship
5150 Highway 22, Suite C-16
Mandeville, LA 70471-2515
(504) 845-1954
www.dickensexchange.com

**New England
Collectibles Exchange**
Bob Dorman
201 Pine Avenue
Clarksburg, MA 01247
(413) 663-3643
www.collectiblesbroker.com

The Village Chronicle
Peter & Jeanne George
757 Park Ave.
Cranston, RI 02910
(401) 467-9343

Villages Classified
Paul & Mirta Burns
P.O. Box 34166
Granada Hills, CA 91394-9166
(818) 368-6765

What The Dickens
Judith Isaacson
2885 West Ribera Place
Tucson, AZ 85742
(520) 297-7019

❄ Insuring Your Collection ❄

As your collection grows in size, so does its value. Insuring you collection is a good idea, since it could be worth hundreds of dollars. You can protect your investment by keeping these three things in mind:

Know your coverage – Collectibles are typically included in homeowners' or renters' insurance policies. Ask your agent if your policy covers fire, theft, floods, hurricanes, tornados, earthquakes and damage or breakage from routine handling. Also, ask if

your policy covers claims at "current replacement value" – the amount it would cost to replace items if they were damaged, lost or stolen – which is extremely important since the secondary market value of some pieces may well exceed their original retail price.

Document your collection – In the event of a loss, you will need a record of the contents and value of your collection along with photographs and video footage with close-up views of each piece. Many companies accept a reputable secondary market price guide – such as the Collector's Value Guide™ – as a valid source for determining your collection's value. Ask your insurance agent what information is acceptable. Keep receipts and an inventory of your collection in a different location, such as a safe-deposit box. Include the purchase date, price paid, size, issue year, edition limit/number, special markings and secondary market value for each piece.

Weigh the risk – To determine the coverage you need, calculate how much it would cost to replace your collection and compare it to the total amount your current policy would pay. To insure your collection for a specific dollar amount, ask your agent about adding a Personal Articles Floater or a Fine Arts Floater or "rider" to your policy, or insuring your collection under a separate policy. As with all insurance, you must weigh the risk of loss against the cost of additional coverage.

Production & Packaging

E ach Snowbabies and Snowbunnies figurine begins with a rough sketch, which is revised and refined by Department 56 artist and illustrator Kristi Jensen Pierro. To show dimension and proportion, Pierro creates a scale drawing that is sent to a sculptor who creates a three-dimensional prototype. A production mold is generated from the sculpture, which is filled with liquid porcelain and fired.

After the porcelain cools, it is sanded and smoothed, details are cemented into place using a clay "slip" mixture and the figurine is kiln-fired at temperatures up to 1250° Fahrenheit. This chemical process, known as reduction, produces a hard, white porcelain. The lips and eyes on every piece is hand painted, and the bisque snow crystals ("nubbies") are carefully applied by hand. The Department 56 logo is stamped into the bottoms of most of the figurines to identify them as original Department 56 products.

From Department 56 To You

Snowbabies figurines are packaged in either dark green "storybook" boxes with gold accents or larger green cardboard boxes. Ornaments and smaller pieces are packaged in green boxes with acetate covers, while pewter miniatures are packaged in white boxes decorated with foil stars.

Snowbunnies figurines also come in cardboard or "storybook" boxes that are white with pink accents. This year, there is new packaging for the Snowbunnies pieces, which feature a grass-green color and flower motif, and a picture of the enclosed piece and its name on the front and bottom of the box. The Easter Collectible figurines are boxed in white packaging with a pink tulip design.

Display Ideas

While many Snowbabies collectors prefer to display their treasured pieces in china and curio cabinets, others have discovered that a little imagination and a few creative touches can put the spotlight on their special pieces from Frosty Frolic Land!

Welcome Home – First impressions are the most lasting ones, so welcome visitors to your home with a unique and stunning wreath featuring your favorite Snow-babies ornaments. Attach five or six ornaments with flexible florist wire at even intervals around an artificial evergreen wreath. Then, place accents of bows between the ornaments and add dried touches of dried baby's breath to complete the wreath.

Let's Go Play Outside! – Because the Snowbabies figurines are often engaged in some wonderful activity, a display can be arranged highlighting their fun. In the display shown below, a day of snowball fights and sledding is captured with pieces frolicking on a blanket of snowy white felt fabric against a winter scene backdrop. Nest, build a cotton mound for the sledders to slide down, and make a snow fort out of sugar cubes to complete the effect.

Just For Baby – If you received some Snowbabies figurines as baby gifts, enjoy them every day on the bureau in your baby's room. Here, the charming musical "Just Follow The Star" coordinates with the four pieces in ". . . And That Spells BABY" – and the soft shades of the pieces blend in with the decor of the nursery.

The Writing Desk – Collections often start with one special piece. Giving it a place of honor is as easy as placing it on your desk where you write letters and pay your bills. The Snowbabies figurine "You Didn't Forget Me" is a good reminder that a personal note is always appreciated and may inspire you to open your address book and reconnect with someone from your past!

A Touch Of Paris – For those of us who have been fortunate enough to travel to France – and for those of us who dream of a Parisian holiday – the Snowbabies figurine "A Gift So Fine From Madeline" from *The Guest Collection* can transport us to Paris every day! To accessorize the figurine, arrange postcards, a travel brochure or map and a picture of the Eiffel Tower with French pastries and a copy of the classic tale "Madeline."

Welcome Spring! – After a long winter season of snowy days and frigid nights, the warmth of springtime is welcomed by Snowbunnies figurines. A cheerful arrangement can be achieved by placing green felt material on a table and adding a few pots of miniature flowers around a pond made of cardboard covered with blue paper or cellophane. Arrange your favorite Snowbunnies pieces to bring springtime indoors at your house!

❄ Gift Ideas Checklist ❄

Snowbabies figurines make wonderful gifts for just about any occasion. Here are some gift ideas for the special people in your life, whether they are animal lovers, sports fans or just celebrating a special day. All of the figurines listed here are current.

Animals

- ❏ Jack Frost . . . Through Frosty Forest (1999, #69020)
- ❏ A Journey For Two, By Caribou! (1998, #68881)
- ❏ Parade Of Penguins (set/6, 1995, #68804)
- ❏ Stuck In The Snow (1998, #68932)

Birthday

- ❏ A Gift For You (*Avon exclusives*, Jan. – Dec., 2000, # 217-468 - 224-102)
- ❏ Make A Wish (1998, #68926)

Celebration

- ❏ Follow Me (LE-2000, 1999, #68944)
- ❏ Jumping For Joy (1999, #69036)
- ❏ Off To A Good Start (*Bachman's exclusive*, 1999, #6859)

Christmas

- ❏ Jingle Bell (1997, #68855)
- ❏ Ring The Bells . . . It's Christmas! (1995, #68764)
- ❏ Thank You (1997, #68857)

Encouragement

- ❏ Even A Small Light Shines In The Darkness (1999, #69017)
- ❏ I Need A Hug (1992, #68136)
- ❏ I'll Light The Way (*Disney exclusive*, 1999, #25430224)
- ❏ Pull Together (1998, #68924)
- ❏ There's No Place Like Home (1996, #68820)

Friendship

- ❏ I Caribou You (1999, #68942)
- ❏ Jolly Friends Forevermore (set/11, 1999, #69021)
- ❏ One For You, One For Me (1997, #68858)
- ❏ Reach For The Moon (*Avon exclusive*, 1999, #254927)
- ❏ To My Friend (1998, #68917)

Love

- ❏ Falling For You (1999, #69035)
- ❏ I Love You This Much! (1998, #68918)
- ❏ I'll Love You Always (*Spring Promotion 2000 event piece*, 1999, #69009)

Music

- ❏ Music From The Highest (set/3, 1999, #69016)
- ❏ Starlight Serenade (1997, #68856)

Nature

- ❏ It's Snowing! (1996, #68821)
- ❏ Heigh-Ho, Heigh-Ho,
  To Frolic Land We Go! (1997, #68853)
- ❏ Starlight, Starbright (1999, #69015)

New Baby

- ❏ . . . And That Spells BABY (set/4, 1998, #68923)
- ❏ I'm So Sleepy (1996, #68810)
- ❏ The Littlest Angel (1999, #69011)
- ❏ Now I Lay Me Down To Sleep (1993, #68390)
- ❏ Read Me A Story! (1990, #79456)
- ❏ You've Got The Cutest Little Baby Face (1998, #68933)

Playtime

- ❏ All Aboard The Star Express (set/4, 1999, #68943)
- ❏ My Snowbaby Baby Dolls (set/2, 1998, #68919)
- ❏ Stargazer's Castle (1998, #68925)
- ❏ When The Bough Breaks (1996, #68819)

Sledding

- ❏ Down The Hill We Go! (1987, #79600)
- ❏ Jack Frost . . . A Sleighride Through The Stars (set/3, 1996, #68811)
- ❏ Slip, Sliding Away (1998, #68934)
- ❏ Two Little Babies On The Go! (1997, #68840)

Snowmen

- ❏ Shake It Up, Baby (1999, #69013)
- ❏ Where Did He Go? (1993, #68411)
- ❏ Why Don't You Talk To Me? (1991, #68012)
- ❏ You Need Wings Too! (1996, #68818)

Sports

- ❏ Batter Up (*Starlight Games*, 1999, #69047)
- ❏ Come Sail With Me (1999, #69019)
- ❏ Hit The Mark (*Starlight Games*, 1999, #69005)
- ❏ I Can Touch My Toes (set/2, 1998, #68927)
- ❏ Over The Top (*Starlight Games*, 1999, #69004)
- ❏ Score (*Starlight Games*, 1999, #69007)
- ❏ Ship O' Dreams (set/2, 1997, #68859)

The Guest Collection

- ❏ A Gift So Fine From Madeline (1998, #69901)
- ❏ I Have A Feeling We're Not In Kansas Anymore (1998, #69900)
- ❏ They're Coming From Oz, Oh My! (1999, #69010)
- ❏ A Kiss For You And 2000 Too (1999, #69902)

❄ Numerical Index ❄

All Snowbabies, Snowbunnies and Easter Collectibles pieces are listed in numerical order by stock number with each piece's location in the Value Guide and the box in which it is pictured.

Numerical Index

✳ Alphabetical Index ✳

All Snowbabies, Snowbunnies and Easter Collectibles pieces are listed in alphabetical order by name with each piece's location in the Value Guide and the box in which it is pictured.

KEY:

FG = figurine
HB = hinged box
LP = lamp
MO = miniature ornament
MU = musical
OR = ornament
PM = pewter miniature
PN = pin
TT = tree topper
VT = votive
WG = waterglobe

Alphabetical Index

127